WORDS'
WORTH

WORDS' WORTH

A HANDBOOK ON WRITING AND SELLING NONFICTION

❑

Terri Brooks

St. Martin's Press
New York

Design by Barbara Bert/North 7 Atelier Ltd.

Library of Congress Cataloging-in-Publication Data

Brooks, Terri.
    Words' worth.

    1. Feature writing. I. Title.
PN4784.F37B76 1989   808'.06607   89-10331
ISBN 0-312-03005-3
ISBN 0-312-03581-0 (ppk.)

First Edition

10 9 8 7 6 5 4 3 2 1

For My Son Brian

CONTENTS

ACKNOWLEDGMENTS

I AM GRATEFUL to many people for their help with various stages of this book.

I owe a debt of gratitude to several colleagues at New York University: especially to David Rubin, who gave me the chance to teach about writing; to my deans, C. Duncan Rice and Ann Burton, for their pragmatic and collegial support; and to many of the members of the Department of Journalism and Mass Communication, for their suggestions and advice during the last five years pertaining to this book.

I was lucky to have good critics early on, and would like to especially acknowledge Judith Daniels, magazine consultant; Kingsley Ervin, Headmaster of Grace Church School; Sara Friedman, vice president, and Alec Dubro, president, of the National Writers' Union; Joseph Byrnes, Professor of English at NYU; and Ann Bevilacqua, of the Elmer Holmes Bobst Library. All critiqued portions of the manuscript.

Thanks also to my NYU colleague and media critic Edwin Diamond; and to James Carey, Dean of the College of

Communications at the University of Illinois for their early reviews, suggestions, and words of encouragement.

Many helped to gather materials from newspapers, books, and magazines to use as examples in the text. Among them, I would particularly like to acknowledge James H. Ottaway, Jr., chairman of Ottaway Newspapers Inc.; Jerry Sass, vice president of education, the Gannett Foundation; Phil Currie, Gannett's vice-president of news for community newspapers; Roy Peter Clark, Dean of the Faculty at the Poynter Institute for Media Studies; Carole Ashkinaze, columnist, editorial writer, and member of the editorial board, at *The Atlanta Journal-Constitution;* Jon Katz and Sonia Robbins, who teach journalism at NYU; Paul Steiger, deputy managing editor at *The Wall Street Journal;* Stewart Kampel, editor of the Long Island Weekly section of the *New York Times;* and Paula Span, staff writer of *The Washington Post.* They tracked down articles, recommended writers, and got me into newspaper libraries.

The editors I have come to know at St. Martin's Press have demonstrated remarkable patience and unfailing good nature: I am particularly indebted to Brian DeFiore, who bought the book; to George Witte, who did the editing; to Mark Gallaher and Cathy Pusateri, who appreciated its possibilities as a college text; and to Marilyn Moller and her son, Willie who provided my introduction to the college division editors. I also thank my agent Charlotte Sheedy, for her faith in the idea.

A special thank-you must go to Janice Burns, for all the weekends and evenings she spent putting this manuscript and its revisions into her computer; to Rondi Charleston, for her meticulous fact checking and research in the final stages of the manuscript; and to Elizabeth Abrams, for her congenial disposition and organizational skills that allowed me to do two full-time jobs at once.

And a long overdue acknowledgment of gratitude and affection goes to Wilmott Ragsdale, my former journalism professor at the University of Wisconsin, who taught thousands of us Midwesterners a true love of language.

On an intimate note, I am forever grateful to Françoise and Sidney Aronson of Mijas, Spain, for providing us with a wonderful place to stay and for their nurturing support while I worked on the first draft; to my mother, Virginia, whose presence in Spain made it possible for me to begin; and to Yasmine Bouali, Sabine Fimbres, Anna Ryan, and Marcia Parris, who cared so creatively and tenderly for my son while I researched and wrote. And thanks, of course, to my son, Brian—patient and understanding far beyond his six years— who already has his own wonderful way with words.

This book is based on my twenty years' work as a newspaper reporter, freelance magazine writer, and book author. It is also based on my experience teaching reporting, feature writing, and magazine writing to students during the last ten years. Dozens of these former students now edit and write for newspapers and magazines across the country. While I would like to think it was their in-class education that led to such success, I find myself constantly humbled and amazed by the way students learn to write. A good student can be taught the essential principles laid out in this book. The best ones go beyond that, drawing on instinct and innate talent to teach the teacher a thing or two about the power and possibilities of words. As a result, I am indebted forever to all my students who tried so hard to "get it right," and sometimes succeeded so magnificently.

This book includes dozens of examples of feature writing to illustrate various points. These examples were gleaned in a most haphazard way: from newspapers I read most frequently or happened to read on a given day; from clips stuffed in my office mailbox; from writers I admire; from editors and publishers who referred me to their own best writers. I would like to acknowledge the publications and writers whose words appear in these pages.

The publications are these:
Associated Press, *Atlanta Journal-Constitution, Baltimore News American, Chicago Daily News, Chicago Tribune, Chronicle-Tribune* (Marion, Ohio), *The Clarion-Ledger* (Jackson, Miss.), *Columbia Journalism Review, The Daily Star* (Oneonta, N.Y.), *The Dallas Morning News, The Denver Post, Detroit Free Press, Esquire, Free Press* (Mankato, Minn.), *Greensboro News & Record* (N.C.), *International Herald Tribune* (Paris, France), *Los Angeles Times, Marietta Daily Journal* (Ga.), *News and Sun-Sentinel* (Fort Lauderdale, Fla.), *Newsday, The New York Times, New Yorker, Philadelphia Inquirer, Quill, Reno Gazette-Journal* (Nev.), *Rockford Register Star* (Ill.), *Rocky Mountain News* (Denver, Colo.), *The Tennessean* (Nashville), *Time, Times-Herald Record* (Middletown, N.Y.), *U.S. News & World Report, Village Voice* (New York, N.Y.), *The Virginian-Pilot* (Norfolk), *The Wall Street Journal, Washington Journalism Review, The Washington Post*.

And the writers are as follows:
Carole Agus, John Andrew, Jim Auchmutey, Felicity Barringer, Robert Barry, Tad Bartimus, Jacques Barzun, Marcia Bates, Mary Blume, Stephen Braun, Ed Breen, Stan Buckles, Stacey Burling, John F. Burns, Bryan Burrough, John Camp, Truman Capote, Raad Cawthon, Roy Peter Clark, Roger Cohen, Alan Cowell, Judith Cummings, Neil Cunningham, Charlotte Curtis, Bob Dart, Angelo DeBernardo, Joan Didion, Annie Dillard, John Aloysius Farrell, Esther B. Fein, Judy Foreman, Catherine Fox, Nicholas Gage, Phil Gailey, William E. Geist, Cynthia Gorney, Keith Graham, Eugene Griffin, Randy Hammer, Art Harris, Ernest Hemingway, Michael Herr, John Hersey, Jan Hoffman, Kathy Trocheck Hogan, David Huddle, Christopher Isherwood, Molly Ivins, Dirk Johnson, Henry Kamm, Joel Kaplan, Elizabeth Kastor, Michael T. Kaufman, James E. Knowles, Edwin A. Lahey, Gerald Lanson, Paula LaRocque, Russell Leavitt, John Leonard, Melissa Ludtke Lincoln, Robert Lindsey, Jules Loh, L. Dupre Long, Norman Mailer, Andrew H. Malcolm, John

McPhee, H. L. Mencken, Ken Miller, Jessica Mitford, Desmond Morris, Beth Mullaly, Brian Ojanpa, George Orwell, Anna Quindlen, Wilmott Ragsdale, Nick Ravo, Alan Riding, Nan Robertson, Dick Roraback, William E. Schmidt, Eric Sevareid, Philip Shabecoff, Nathaniel Sherrard Jr., Timothy K. Smith, Mitchell Stephens, Wesley Stout, Robert Suro, Susan Thomas, Robert Thurow, Greta Tilley, Guy Trebay, Tom Vesey, Ken Wells, David Wiessler, Jim Wilkerson, Tom Wolfe, Marianne Yen, William Zinsser.

WORDS'
WORTH

THE HEALTH OF NONFICTION

THIS BOOK IS ABOUT the kind of nonfiction generally known as feature writing. The term "feature" covers a wide range of nonfiction writing: profiles and portraits of the odd, the famous, the obscure; investigative reporting; sidebars to hard-news stories; service articles; "how-to" stories; travel writing. Features also vary in length—from a few hundred words in a newspaper to thousands of words in a magazine or book. Whatever the subject and medium, the common denominator of features is that they are usually about current issues; they involve careful reporting and research, and they depend on the strength of their writing to get themselves read.

Until recently, feature stories have had a reputation for being the soft underbelly of the news, as if they could not compete with the hard-muscled facts of newspaper journalism. But now hard-core journalists treat feature writing with more respect, and have even begun to absorb its techniques into the basic telling of the news. The truth is that features often work harder than news stories, for they add depth and perspective

1

to events that too often seem arbitrary and serendipitous. They anchor the flight of events. And, since every feature has a "voice," the feature can go where hard news dare not tread, to reveal ethical and moral implications behind a breaking story. Today the best front-page stories incorporate more components of the feature: description, anecdotes, an engaging lead, lively verbs, and language made compelling not only because of the information conveyed but also because of the words used to convey it.

In the 1960s, upstart nonfiction writers such as Tom Wolfe and Gay Talese and Jimmy Breslin and Hunter S. Thompson began to use techniques of fiction to tell their stories of fact. This communion of fact and fiction came to be called the "New Journalism" (although in fact James Boswell in the 1790s and Charles Dickens in the 1800s, among others, also used fictional devices in their reporting) and elevated the status of nonfiction writing. What began as a frenzy of experimentation has matured slowly through two decades into some dazzling nonfiction writing.

Threats to the Craft

Although the status of the feature has risen, it faces continual threats from two fronts. First, despite the creative infusions of the 1960s, too many magazine features continue to be bland in style and predictable in content. This sorry state is exacerbated by merger mania. Twenty-three companies now own the 184 largest circulation magazines, and many of these companies own large newspaper chains as well. Each magazine under a corporate umbrella tends to be specialized, focusing on computers, or money, or health, for instance. Its advertising is aimed at a specific market. Its editors assign stories to appeal to that market.

As a result, there is less and less room for innovation in feature writing. It is rare for an editor of any major magazine to encourage writers to experiment with form or to be bold in subject matter. The editorial bottom line is all too often not "What should our readers know?" but "What will our readers accept?"

One popular women's magazine, for instance, knows that most of its readers are under forty, live in suburbs and small towns, primarily in the Midwest and the South, and have husbands and young children. Its editors would not publish articles that challenge the life-styles of this audience, such as "When Is It Better to Get a Divorce?" or "The Benefits of an Extramarital Affair." And for this magazine, every topic, no matter how potentially tragic, needs to have a hopeful tone and an upbeat ending. Successful contributors know all this, and write to formula.

Besides this economic pressure for predictable prose, declining educational emphasis on the rules of basic grammar is leading to sloppy use of language. This threatens the quality of writing in all genres. By the time students leave elementary school, the damage has already been done. Most disconcerting, studies show that today's teachers even reward purple prose. In a series of experiments with high school and college English teachers during a six-year period, two Chicago researchers found that the teachers consistently preferred verbosity to succinctness. The researchers concluded that this problem of "prolixity" now infests all written and verbal communication. "In the languages of law, medicine, education, government and the social sciences, our tongues have become more voluble, our terms more abused, our sentences yet more false and florid," they concluded.[1]

This indifference to the structural principles and creative possibilities of language leads to a lack of curiosity about the power of English. An alarming proportion of college students—including those in liberal arts programs—manages to devise a plan of study that circumvents most of the classics of English: from the King James version of the Bible to Chaucer and Dickens, up through twentieth-century authors like H. L. Mencken, Lillian Ross, E. B. White, and John McPhee. They've seen the movie, but they've never read the book.

They don't seek out the kind of prose that makes you laugh while sitting all alone in your room, that sends a shiver up your spine from the thrill of a sentence perfectly shaped, or a paragraph beautifully molded and shining out from the page like a small work of art. They do not give themselves the gift of graceful prose like this, from Annie Dillard's *Pilgrim at Tinker Creek:*

> One day I was walking along Tinker Creek thinking of nothing at all and I saw the tree with the lights in it. I saw the backyard cedar where the mourning doves roost charged and transfigured, each cell buzzing with flame. I stood on the grass with the lights in it, grass that was wholly fire, utterly focused and utterly dreamed. It was less like seeing than like being for the first time seen, knocked breathless by a powerful glance. . . . I had been my whole life a bell, and never knew it until at that moment I was lifted and struck.[2]

Or stark prose like this, from Truman Capote's *In Cold Blood:*

> Until one morning in mid-November of 1959, few Americans—in fact, few Kansans—had ever heard of Holcomb. Like the waters of the river, like the motorists on the highway, and like the yellow trains streaking down the Santa Fe tracks, drama, in the shape of exceptional happenings, had never stopped there. The inhabitants of the village, numbering two hundred and seventy, were satisfied that this should be so, quite content to exist inside ordinary life—to work, to hunt, to watch television, to attend school socials, choir practice, meetings of the 4-H Club. But then, in the earliest hours of that morning in November, a Sunday morning, certain foreign sounds impinged on the normal nightly Holcomb noises—on the keening hysteria of coyotes, the dry scrape of scuttling tumbleweed, the racing, receding, wail of locomotive whistles. At the time, not a soul in sleeping Holcomb heard them—four shotgun blasts that, all told, ended six human lives.[3]

In every other profession—whether it be the craft of the carpenter or the research of the physicist—neophytes study the body of work upon which they must build. But too many nonfiction writers, unaware of the grand legacy of their field—a legacy that dates back 2,400 years to Thucydides's coverage of the Peloponnesian War in the fifth century B.C.—are content to build their careers helter-skelter on the sands of popular culture. Without roots, their work does not blossom and thrive.

Ways to Strengthen Your Writing

If you want to become a strong and compelling nonfiction writer, as opposed to simply "another" writer, here are ten basic ground rules:

1. Become Fluent in English Grammar.   Read and memorize William Strunk and E. B. White's *Elements of Style.* [4] Take a course in grammar. Grammar is the foundation of all communication. It is the linguistic face you present to the world. It affects every thought you think, every word you speak or write. While the suggestions in this book are tailored for feature writing in newspapers and magazines, the same principles apply to term papers, corporate reports, press releases, job applications, speeches, and letters home. Your mother, however, will forgive an error of grammar or syntax; editors and potential employers will not.

2. Draw Up a Reading List.   Create a list that will educate, not just entertain, you. Mix fiction and nonfiction. Mix the classics and the new; the popular and the esoteric. Let your reading cover a wide range of material from Shakespeare's *Macbeth* to poems by Walt Whitman and John Ashbery; from Flannery O'Connor's short stories, to Sir Arthur Conan Doyle's *Complete Sherlock Holmes.* You will like some books, be mystified by some, turned off by others. Just keep reading. The point is to know what's been written. Then you can fine tune your reading to explore in greater depth certain kinds and styles of writing. To begin a reading list, ask teachers, parents, librarians, and colleagues for the names of their favorite books. Or you can begin with the reading list at the end of this book, then adapt it as you wish. (See "Read Well to Write Well," p.207) Read intelligently, critically, and alertly. Do not read when the television is on, or when you are tired or otherwise distracted. Match wits with the author.

3. Read with a Pencil.   Mark passages that you find especially well written or riveting, and return to them for a second reading after you have finished the article, the chapter, or the book. (If you are reading a borrowed book, make note of the pages to which you want to return.)

Reread the passages analytically and try to pinpoint what makes them "work." Look at the way the author uses the elements of grammar. Are the verbs active or passive? Are they lean and spare, or baroque? Does the author favor adjectives? Adverbs? How do all these choices affect the "style" of the writing? Is the author writing in the first person or third person? Why do you think the author chose to do so? How often does the author use description, anecdotes, quotes? Do they add or detract from the story? How does sentence length affect your reaction to a given paragraph? Choose one paragraph or chapter that you especially like, and look at all these elements in it, picking out one or two simple techniques that the author uses to good effect. Remember those stylistic devices the next time you sit down to write, and try one of them in your own prose.

4. Read with a Dictionary.   Look up words you don't know. Make it a habit to learn at least one new word each time you read.

5. If You Begin to Read Something that Doesn't Appeal to You, Put it Down and Start Another Book. Half the joy of reading is to discover the right book at the right time. But don't abandon a book. If you find it difficult or tedious, read only five to ten pages at a sitting. Or put it away, and try it again from time to time. It is especially difficult to appreciate books that are "assigned" reading. A student in my Literature of Journalism class complained that he found one assignment, Annie Dillard's *Pilgrim at Tinker Creek,* cloying and irrelevant. I agreed—it was a tough book to appreciate in the heart of New York City. I suggested he put it away and take it with him some day when he was going to, say, a remote Greek island. Two years later, he showed up in my office. He had just returned, he said, from a remote Greek island. There, he had read the book and he confided it was "the most wonderful thing I have ever read."

6. Write on a Regular Basis. Like an athlete who can stay in shape only by practicing his or her sport, a writer can stay in shape only by writing. Set aside a few hours each day, or each week. Assign yourself different topics to write about—a recent vacation, an incident on the street, a conversation with a friend. The point is to develop the habit of collecting information and converting it into accurate and graceful prose. Writing is 99 percent sweat equity: those who diligently work at it on a regular basis are most likely to succeed.

7. Choose a Wide Range of Subjects to Write About. This will give you a sense of your strengths and weaknesses as a writer. Begin by going to a local park or shopping mall and taking notes on all you see and hear. Then try to shape your notes into a coherent story. Next, interview someone with an unusual occupation or hobby—from sky diver to podiatrist— and write up the interview. From there, you might cover a local trial, or a community controversy—a story that involves speaking to people on different sides of an issue. Cast a wide net for subjects—from the homeless to an art show. Variety will test your skills as a reporter and writer.

8. Travel. The more you know about the world and the habits of its people, the better writer you will be. As you travel, take notes and keep daily diaries.

9. Every Few Years, Study Something New. Be a lifelong student of history, politics, business, philosophy, languages, the sciences.

10. Be Willing to Fail. For each "success"—whether literary or financial—even the most successful writer can list a half-dozen failures. Failure is a crucial and continual part of the learning process. Knowledge of your own limits and weaknesses is an important step toward developing and refining your strengths. Have the courage to keep writing.

As you read this book, keep in mind George Orwell's advice about writing—offered to writers more than forty years ago, but even more valid today.

> What is above all needed is to let the meaning choose the word, and not the other way about. In prose, the worst thing one can do with words is to surrender to them. . . . Probably it is better to put off using words as long as possible and get one's meaning as clear as one can through pictures or sensations. Afterwards one can choose—not simply *accept*—the phrases that will best cover the meaning, and then switch round and decide what impression one's words are likely to make on another person. This last effort of the mind cuts out all stale or mixed images, all prefabricated phrases, needless repetitions, and humbug and vagueness generally. But one can often be in doubt about the effect of a word or a phrase, and one needs rules that one can rely on when instinct fails. I think the following rules will cover most cases:

   i. Never use a metaphor, simile or other figure of speech which you are used to seeing in print.

   ii. Never use a long word where a short one will do.

  iii. If it is possible to cut a word out, always cut it out.

  iv. Never use the passive where you can use the active.

   v. Never use a foreign phrase, a scientific word or a jargon word if you can think of an everyday English equivalent.

  vi. Break any of these rules sooner than say anything outright barbarous.

These rules sound elementary, and so they are, but they demand a deep change of attitude in anyone who has grown used to writing in the style now fashionable.[5]

❏ A SELF-TEST FOR WRITERS

Here are twenty-five common traits of good writers. Read them carefully. At least twenty-three of them should apply to you if you plan to pursue a profession in nonfiction writing.[6] (Well, twenty-two will do.)

Common Traits of Good Writers

1. The world is their journalism laboratory.
2. If they can get out of the office, they can find a story.
3. They prefer to discover and develop their own story ideas.
4. They take notes like crazy.
5. They are voracious collectors of information.
6. They spend too much time and energy working on their leads.
7. Because they care about endings, it's almost impossible to cut their stories from the bottom.
8. They rehearse their stories constantly, eating lunch, driving in cars, brushing their teeth.
9. Most are bleeders—agonizing over each word and sen-

tence—rather than speeders. But they are versatile enough to speed when they have to.

10. They immerse themselves in the story; they live it.
11. They understand that a part of writing is the mechanical drudgery of organizing the material.
12. They appreciate collaboration with good editors, but spend more time avoiding bad editors and what they perceive to be useless assignments.
13. They rewrite.
14. Because they see imperfections, many hate to read their own published work.
15. They are in constant search of the human side of the news.
16. They have an eye for the offbeat.
17. They have confidence in their readers.
18. They tend to be sympathetic toward the people they write about.
19. They take chances in their writing.
20. Their writing has "voice"—the illusion of someone talking directly to the reader.
21. They think a lot about quotations: how to get them, how to use them.
22. They are lifelong readers, mostly of novels.
23. They write too long and know it.
24. All writing, for them, is autobiographical.
25. They love words.

□ 1 □

THE LEAD

IN A HARD-NEWS STORY, the standard *inverted pyramid* lead still wears well: the most important five *W*'s appear first—Who, What, When, Where, Why—with the remaining information presented in descending order of importance. This "just the facts" approach to reporting fires, wars, murders, stock market plunges, and the other nitty-gritty upon which newspapers thrive serves up the news quickly and clearly. It also allows editors to chop a story from the bottom if it runs too long.

But the lead for a feature story—whether in a newspaper or a magazine—imposes other demands on the writer. It must lure the reader into a story that he or she might otherwise ignore.

Feature leads are tough to write; they need to be wrestled to the mat. If not kept in control, they tend to degenerate into turgid prose, leaving the reader slogging through Jell-O journalism before finally reaching a salient fact.

Consider this array of failed leads, compiled by two colleagues:

The Tasteless. On a story about an infant abandoned just before New Year's Day: "While most people were preparing to ring out the old, someone rang out the new this week . . ."

The Puzzling. On a rate-hike story: "The old saying that the grass is always greener on the other side of the fence isn't necessarily true when it comes to utility rates."

The Absurd. About an ethnic community: "Cleveland Ukrainians know great strides are taken in little steps."[1]

The trick is to be clever and creative, without being schmaltzy or sloppy, as above. Also avoid worn-out clichés, predictable puns that make people groan, platitudes, and bad language generally. Remember that the lead is the key that unlocks the feature story. It should hold promise, should intrigue and tantalize. Keep in mind, too, that most people read a feature to the end not *because* of the subject, but *despite* it. It is not the content of the story, but the way in which the story is presented, that infuses it with life or condemns it to death.

How long should your lead be? In briefer features of up to 1,500 words, the lead may run from one sentence to three paragraphs in length. Avoid longer leads when possible (and it is usually possible). Don't waste space with a windy hello. And keep in mind that most brief features appear in newspapers or "special interest" sections of magazines, and are often squeezed into narrow columns. In this format, short paragraphs and leads are easier on the eyes and less daunting to readers.

Save longer leads for longer magazine articles. First, the reader will know this is a "long read" and be more willing to settle into a good lead without losing patience. Second, magazine graphics tend to include more white space, wider columns, and more art, so the eye is not besieged by a dense black mass of type. But don't dawdle with your lead, no matter what your story's length. Make every word work.

Obviously, every lead is uniquely tailored to fit the story it introduces. In that sense, there are as many kinds of leads as there are features to be written. But most of these leads can be identified as one of six basic varieties:

1. Anecdotal
2. Descriptive
3. Quote
4. Summation
5. Tease
6. Zinger

The kind you choose is to some extent predetermined by the subject, and your point of view toward that subject. (See chapter 6, "Voice" for more on point of view.) A feature should not only inform, but also evoke reaction. It should be touching, sad, funny, wistful, annoying, intriguing, outrageous, revolting. It should aim to elicit any of the constellations of emotion that reflect human foibles, failings, fascinations, and frustrations. The success of your chosen lead depends on your diligence as a writer, your patience, your instincts about what will work best, and, to some extent, your good luck in finally striking just the right chord. The longer you work at it, the better your odds.

Anecdotal

The anecdotal lead draws the reader into the feature with a mini-narration. This gives the writer a chance to tell a small, revealing story that reflects the larger story at hand.

EXAMPLE 1:

The coverage of disaster—whether earthquake, war, flood, or disease—is most effective when it spotlights the impact on one person, one family. Here is an anecdotal lead to one of the many features on people with Acquired Immune Deficiency Syndrome (AIDS).

> The night before his high school class reunion, the telephone rang for Dean Lechner.
>
> A classmate he had known since kindergarten was calling on behalf of the reunion organizing committee, she said, to tell him not to come.
>
> "If you come," she warned, "people will leave." And for the first time since Mr. Lechner had been diagnosed as having AIDS, he sat down and cried.[2]

Why it Works: If a feature contains conflict between two or more opposing camps, an example of that tension can be shaped into an effective anecdotal lead. In this case, a moment of confrontation crystallizes the drama of the entire story: how a person with AIDS is treated by one neighbor in the small Minnesota hometown to which he returns to live and die.

The writer freezes a moment in time and space: a man at home one evening, a ringing telephone, a hostile message. The writer sketches *just enough* detail: why the night is significant (it's before the class reunion); who the caller is (a classmate known since kindergarten); what the message is (we don't want you); how the person with AIDS reacts (tears). The lead is pared to the basics: superfluous material is deliberately left out. The author could have, for instance, inserted more quotes, more description, more background. But by keeping it short and simple, it becomes more stark and powerful.

The way in which each sentence is written also enhances the tension intrinsic in the story itself. Each sentence starts "soft" cushioned by a clause or phrase, and builds to the hard, cold facts of the ringing telephone, the message, the tears. The drama of rejection mounts paragraph by paragraph. And because the incident is presented only from the victim's point of view—it is his telephone ringing, his response—rather than from the caller's point of view, the lead also engages the reader's sympathies on behalf of Mr. Lechner.

EXAMPLE 2:

An anecdote need not always be current to qualify for the lead. A glimpse from the past can set the scene for a current drama. This lead goes back in history to dramatize the poignancy of the present.

> In May 1979, Police Officer Anthony J. Abruzzo Jr. was dispatched to a fire on Main Street in Flushing, Queens.
>
> In the course of crowd control, he found himself repeatedly warning a young woman with hair to her waist and enormous doe eyes to stay back at a safe distance on the other side of the street. Officer Abruzzo soon went from giving the young woman orders to asking her questions. He found out that her name was Barbara and that she worked in a furniture store on the street. A few days later, he came back to look for her.
>
> Yesterday Barbara Abruzzo remembered that. She was sitting in the basement of the 109th Precinct station house drinking coffee while her husband's colleagues eddied around her, waiting to load their paper plates with cold cuts. She had just finished unveiling a bronze plaque emblazoned with Tony Abruzzo's profile and his shield.
>
> "No Greater Devotion to Sworn Duty Can a Police Officer Demonstrate to God and to Man Than to Lay Down His Life in the Line of Duty," it said on the plaque.[3]

Why it Works: This lead is a gentle, understated narration of love and its tragic end. The anecdote about their first meeting could be tightened—it is not snappy. But it has a quiet, unpretentious poignancy that reflects the people in the story itself.

Events are made to seem beyond human control here. The verbs are subdued, tentative, passive: the police officer "was dispatched"; he "found himself repeatedly warning" his future wife; he "went from giving orders to asking questions." The widow is "sitting"; she "remembers"; her husband's colleagues "wait." The strongest verb—"eddied"—reinforces the feeling of a current pulling people along.

It is as if we are glimpsing a scene through an open door—uninvited witnesses to tragedy. The action here is already complete: Anthony J. Abruzzo Jr. was long ago murdered; the plaque has been unveiled. The sorrow here is inarticulate: no one is quoted directly. The single quote comes not from the mute mourners, but from the plaque itself—objective, stark, final.

Descriptive

"One good word is worth a thousand pictures," Eric Sevareid once told Charles Kurault. Kurault agreed. It was high praise, indeed, coming from two picture-oriented television journalists. The descriptive lead is that "one good word," the verbal photograph that captures the essence of a person, a place, an event. While the anecdotal lead moves the story forward through time, the descriptive lead anchors the story in place. The challenge to the writer is to find the description that can symbolize an entire story. The good descriptive lead, like the anecdotal lead, is a powerful way to enter a story.

EXAMPLE 1:

Here is the lead to a profile of U.S. chess champion, Yasser Seirawan.

> He is hale, hip and handsome. He swims, skis, surfs. His forehand, they say, is as devastating in karate as it is in tennis.

He is a hustler, a snorkeler and a notorious ladies' man, surfacing a few years back as Cosmopolitan's "Bachelor of the Month." He even reads, voraciously.

On the side, Yasser Seirawan plays a little chess.[4]

Why it Works: The writer picks out the traits that set this man apart from the stereotypical chess player, to let the reader know this is no run-of-the-mill international grand master. He then lists these traits in a simple, clear way. The first two sentences are brisk and breezy, like the man they are describing.

The writer also takes advantage of three literary techniques used almost instinctively by feature writers, all of them involving different kinds of *repetition.*

First, *alliteration.* The repetition of the first consonant sounds in a series of neighboring words—in this case, the *h*'s and *s*'s—gives an appealing singsong quality to this lead.

Second, *chains of description.* In this case, trilogies of adjectives (hale, hip, handsome); verbs (swims, skis, surfs); and nouns (hustler, snorkeler, ladies' man) set up a rhythm that helps to "swing" the reader forward into the story. This technique of linking a series of (often, three) words, phrases, or dependent clauses gives fullness and texture to an otherwise flat sentence.

And third, *parallel sentence structure.* Each of the first five sentences begins with the pronoun "he" or "his," in most cases followed quickly by the verb. This repetition of structure in the independent clauses also helps create forward momentum in a story.

However, avoid overrepetition. This lead works so well in part because the repetition is broken up momentarily in the third sentence with the intrusion of the clause "they say," and in the fourth sentence with the addition of the phrase "surfacing a few years back . . ." each of which gives readers a chance to catch their breath.

Note, too, that the writer uses adverbs sparingly. The

only one—"voraciously"—stands out not only because it is used in an unusual context (as if Seirawan "devours" his books) but also because it is saved for the very last word in the paragraph. He lets his adjectives, verbs, and nouns do the rest of the work.

EXAMPLE 2:

This lead introduces a feature on the despair felt by the victims of a prolonged civil war.

> South of Beirut, a 16-year-old Druze warrior, his long hair held away from his face by a red band, puts down his rifle, blows some bubble gum and surveys what is left of the village of Kfar Matta.
>
> What is left is a large expanse of rubble, dotted with tires, 7Up cans, an Adidas running shoe and other relics of ordinary life. Here and there is a home that hasn't been completely destroyed, its interior exposed to the dusty wind.[5]

Why it Works: The description begins with a close-up (the boy), then moves to a wide angle (a large expanse of rubble) and ends with a panoramic sweep (the ruined home, the dusty wind)—much in the manner of a film sequence. By building this barren scene around one person, the writer finds a way to humanize an otherwise faceless and distant tragedy.

The first paragraph also packs in a lot of information. In one sentence, we learn where we are (south of Beirut, in a village called Kfar Matta), who we are with (a Druze warrior, age 16), something of what he looks like (long hair, a red band, holding a rifle), and what he is doing (blowing bubble gum, looking around).

In the beginning of the second sentence, with the repetition of the phrase "what is left," the writer moves the reader "inside" the boy's own vision, which keeps the story personal. He then highlights the "ordinary" things any teenager such as this one might notice first: tires, 7-Up cans, a single Adidas shoe.

The final sentence, even though it sweeps the scene, also manages to stay personal by referring to the single home "here and there," left partially standing. If instead the writer had written: "Most homes were completely destroyed," it would have depersonalized the moment, for the human psyche is unable to cope with massive devastation with the same compassion that it can handle one individual tragedy. This is why a descriptive, focused lead such as this one is useful for easing readers into a story about any large-scale disaster or trauma.

The writer also uses the juxtaposition of opposites as an effective literary device. This juxtaposition creates a symbolism that goes below the surface detail of the things described to a deeper and unarticulated level. The image of the "warrior" blowing bubble gum; of a popular brand of American running shoe in the rubble of a foreign battlefield; of the privacy of homes ripped open to swirling dust and the eyes of strangers—each symbolizes the different levels at which this culture has been ripped apart.

Quote

This kind of lead is used far more often than it should be, by writers who have given up on the lead and decide to throw in a quote just to get the story started. From time to time, however, the perfect, irresistible quote comes along that seems a natural for the lead. If you use direct quotes, it is best to keep them short. If the quotes run long, be sure they are carefully interspersed with description—however brief to break them up. And remember that one of the sures' to kill a feature is to lean on quotes—to overquote— in the lead or in the body of the story. (See "Quotes.")

EXAMPLE 1:

Here is the lead to a feature on driving lessons in the city.

> "I would suggest," Bob Kousoulos says calmly to his driving student, Jules, "that you do something soon with the brakes. It is a red light, Jules."
>
> "Jules, the brakes!"
>
> Mr. Kousoulos, who has been teaching driving for 12 years and is a veteran of thousands of driving missions on the streets of New York, chain-smokes Marlboros, chuckles nervously and tries to maintain a veneer of calm.
>
> "This pedestrian in the middle of the street," Mr. Kousoulos says softly as the vehicle picks up speed after the light, "has apparently decided to end it all. I know you have the right of way, Jules, but let her go, Jules—let her go!"
>
> "Jules," he says, as the student driver weaves his way tensely through pedestrians crossing against the lights, through fields of potholes, numerous construction projects, bicyclists, triple-parked cars and other obstacles that make up the New York motoring experience, "I am sure that this man ahead likes his car, that he would prefer you not hit his car."
>
> "Get into the next lane, Jules. Please!"[6]

Why it Works: This on-the-scene monologue effectively conveys the stress and humor of the situation. Through these one-sided quotes (we never hear the student's responses—he is the foil for this comedy routine) the reader senses barely averted disaster.

But good quotes need a good support system to be effective. This has it. *Punctuation* and *paragraphing* play a big role in pacing the monologue to heighten tension and humor: commas, exclamation marks, and a dash all make it feel as if the reader as well as the car is moving ahead in jerky fits and starts. And the two truncated paragraphs, each containing a single alarmist quote ("Jules, the brakes!" and "Get into the next lane, Jules. Please!") are like brakes themselves, pulling the reader up short before lurching ahead to the next crisis.

Description is placed strategically to highlight the quotes and the tension. At each crisis, the ongoing quote is interrupted by description—the teacher chain-smoking, the car speeding up, the obstacles in the road—leaving the reader suspended briefly in the face of near disaster.

The descriptions themselves are vivid, to-the-point. They are the setting in which the jeweled quotes are placed, and each description is intended to enhance the impact of the quote. Specific word choice also lends a tragicomic effect. The teacher is a "veteran" of "missions," as in war. This is "the New York motoring experience," which sounds straight out of a 1920s tourist guide. In addition, the repetition of the student's name—seven times in this brief space—emphasizes the frazzled nerves of the anxious instructor.

EXAMPLE 2:

One advantage of quotes is that they can take the reader directly to the heart of a story, into the most bizarre and private corners of the soul, without seeming to be intrusive.

Here is the quote leading to a story of a private paramilitary training camp for mercenaries.

> "I want to talk to you today," Frank Camper says, "about removing ears."
>
> Mr. Camper, surrounded by his bruised and bandaged students, demonstrates the slap, grip and downward twist that is the recommended method for separating an ear from its owner during a fight. "After you've got it, the man won't believe it," Mr. Camper says. "So take a step back . . . and show it to him."[7]

Why it Works: An act that to most people is abhorrent, to this man is a matter of pride. For this reason, the author apparently couldn't resist using it in the lead. In this case, it was appropriate: the lead was but the first of many examples of the camp's gung-ho enthusiasm for brutality. But if you use a "shocker" quote such as this, be sure it is a fair reflection of the tone and information in the rest of the story.

Summation

The summation lead is comparable to a hard-news lead because it gives the basic information up front. Like the direct quote lead, it may be a sign that the feature writer simply gave up on finding a more creative way into the story. Sometimes, however, it is a simple and effective way to begin.

EXAMPLE 1:

In the children's clothing industry, there's a lot more to sexual identity than pink and blue. Starting with sleepsuits for the newborn, a child's gender is broadcast by a full code of design details. A former freelance designer for Babytogs, which distributes in K-Marts across America, cited some examples: "Round collar for a girl, pointed for a boy. Scalloped edges—never on a boy. For appliques, trains and soldiers for boys, never flowers. A cat is a girl, a dog is a boy. Butterflies girls. Hot dogs are for boys, and ice cream cones for girls. And the bottom line is—Never Put Fruit on a Boy's Garment."[8]

Why it Works: Because the subject matter itself is about a frivolous and arbitrary practice, it is almost as if the author is determined not to succumb to the same frivolity. This is, in fact, written in a tone similar to that used to cover fashion shows: here's what's new on the scene this season. And because the lead (and the story itself) is written in such matter-of-fact hard-news style, it highlights the absurdity of the subject matter.

When using a summation lead, remember to follow the same rules used by hard-news reporters. Tell the reader immediately what the story is about, clearly and concisely. Be direct. Work on the language, so it is clear but also as creative as possible without interfering with the content. Use interesting verbs (here, "broadcast" is a good example). And when necessary, back up the information with a quote or partial quote, and with examples (here, the writer managed to combine both in a quote).

EXAMPLE 2:

One advantage of a summation lead is that it allows you to massage words to fit the subject (for more on this, see chapter 6, "Voice.") The tone of this lead on a country singer in rural Georgia reflects the down-home persona of the subject himself.

> This here's the ballad of Vic Waters.
> Ol' Vic is a red-bearded, shrimp-eating, guitar-picking poet who lives by a bend in the Sapelo River and chronicles the goings-on of McIntosh County down on the Georgia Coast.[9]

Why it Works: The y'all drawl in this lead tells us as much as the facts conveyed about the story to come. It is important, however, not to go overboard when quoting colloquialisms or slang: a little bit goes a long way. Only three local homespun phrases are needed to get across the point that this is about a Southern Boy: "this here's," "ol' Vic," and "goings-on."

Besides using local speech patterns, the writer also takes advantage of the lead to pick up the *rhythms* of the ballad form; the first sentence sounds like it should be accompanied by a twanging guitar. Its pithy descriptions of the man himself, and the specifics of where he lives—on the Sapelo River, in McIntosh County, on the Georgia Coast—evoke echoes of bittersweet country music.

Tease

Some leads that pack the biggest wallop contain a conundrum, an intentional ambiguity, a puzzle, an insinuation.

Tease leads move the reader obliquely into the story with

puns, double entendres, or a new twist to a cliché. They often take longer to write, but they will give your feature a running start.

EXAMPLE 1:

Here is a lead on a story about a narcotics detective in Mason, Ohio, whose undercover identity was discovered by local drug dealers.

Ten days ago, Gary Smith's nightmare came true.[10]

Why it Works: This is both an intriguing play off the more usual line that someone's "dream came true" and a threat intended to strike responsive chords of fear in the reader. Nightmares should come "to life" only in movies or books. What happens when they intrude on real life? The reader needs to read on to find out.

EXAMPLE 2:

In the end, Bill Witthoeft couldn't even give it away.
  He tried dusk-to-dawn features and they stayed home.
  He tried two-for-one discount nights and they stayed home.
  He tried Veterans Nights, Sweetheart Nights, and any other kind of "night" he could think of. And they still stayed home.
  In the end, things even got absurd at New Ulm's Starlite Drive-In.
  "We offered two movies for $1.99 and people complained about getting a penny back. They said, 'Keep it,' " the drive-in manager said.[11]

Why it Works: This feature about the closing of a drive-in movie theater draws the reader bit by bit into the story, offering in each sentence yet one more hint about what this man could not give away. Rather than begin at the beginning, the writer begins with the conclusion ("In the end, Bill Witthoeft couldn't even give it away"), a clever structural device around which he can then weave the rest of his story. (See chapter 7, "The Weave," for more on this.) The writing is crisp and uncluttered, and the tale of chronic frustration is highlighted by repeating key phrases ("he tried," "they stayed home," in the end").

Zinger

The zinger lead, which usually appears on light, humorous stories, is, like the tease, hard to write but satisfying to read. And like the tease, it often includes a massaging of the language into some slightly new configuration. Its unique quality is that it always includes a one-two punch. The reader is first set up, then nailed with a clever line.

One classic zinger lead appeared in the Chicago *Daily News* after criminal Richard Loeb was stabbed to death in prison by an inmate whose favors he had been soliciting. The story began: "Richard Loeb, who was a master of the English language, today ended a sentence with a proposition."[12]

The lead, though it does qualify as tasteless, remains irresistible to punsters and grammarians alike.

EXAMPLE 1:

The Setup:

Some of Beverly Harrell's friends are concerned that she is going to ruin her reputation.

The Punch:

Not because she is a madam who runs a bustling brothel here, but because she is getting into politics.[13]

Why it Works: This lead, about the owner of a Nevada brothel who was running for the state legislature, plays subtly with the old adage that prostitution is the world's oldest profession and politics the world's second oldest. It also addresses the continuing American ambivalence about whether politics is a respectable calling. The writer distances himself from this particular play on words by attributing the sentiments in the lead to Harrell's "friends," rather than taking the burden of it upon himself.

Indeed, when a statement is debatable, controversial, litigious, or a matter of personal perception or taste, it is often the safer route to find someone else to say it for you. You can then attribute it to a named individual (which is preferable), or to an anonymous source, or you can use a blanket attribution, as this author did.

While more commonly used on humorous features, the zinger can be effective on serious stories as well. It can convey impending doom and heighten the poignancy of tragedy.

EXAMPLE 2:

The Setup:

On autumn days, when the flaming aspen lit the nearby foothills golden, Christopher Mastalski did magical things with a football on the playing fields of Centaurus High School.

He had that special mix of talent that the good running backs share: strength, balance, speed and an elegant grace.

Had all gone well, 18-year-old Chris Mastalski would have played football for the University of Colorado next fall. Coach Chuck Fairbanks' staff ranked him among the top 20 prospects in the state.

The Punch:

Instead, the young athlete died Tuesday from knife wounds he had received the night before.[14]

Why it Works: Here, the lead dramatizes the contrast between the promise of vibrant youth and the tragedy of violent death. The writer introduces this profile with the imagery of life—flaming aspens, golden foothills, gifted athletic ability, elegant grace. The writer immediately makes us feel we would like this young man if we knew him, and this lure to familiarity is heightened when he refers to the subject first by his more formal name, Christopher, and then, in the third paragraph, by his nickname, Chris.

But from the beginning, juxtaposed with all this vitality, are the verbs marshaled so relentlessly in the past tense, which convey a sense of doom.

Both the promise and the threat are there. And, in the fifth sentence, he takes away the young man, forever—that single, final fact cutting starkly across the page. The lead serves the story well, for it evokes first a glow of health and bounty, and then a shock of outrage, leaving us bereft.

❑ LEAD EXERCISES

1. How are you at writing leads? Clip a feature story of 2,000 words or less from your local or state newspaper's life-style or Sunday magazine section. Then address the following questions:

  • What kind of lead is on the story?
  • Does it "work"? If so, why? If not, why not?
  • How could it be improved?
  • Write five new leads for the story.
  • Which of the five works best? Why?

2. Find and clip from newspapers and magazines six feature stories with the six kinds of leads described in this chapter (anecdotal, descriptive, quote, summation, tease, zinger).

- If you feel the lead is effective, analyze why, based on the analyses in this chapter.
- If the lead is weak, rewrite it to make it better. You may alter the existing lead, or write an entirely new one.

3. Clip a hard-news story of at least 500 words from your newspaper of choice and write three good feature leads for this story.

□ 2 □
TRANSITIONS

TRANSITIONS ARE THE WORDS or phrases at the beginning of each paragraph that link one thought to the next. They sometimes occur within paragraphs as well, to link two sentences with disparate thoughts.

If transitions are successful, they lead the reader painlessly through the most complex story. If transitions are inadequate, inappropriate, or nonexistent, the reader will feel befuddled and lost. When you need to reread an article, or parts of it, again and again to understand what is going on, the culprit may well be weak or ineffective transitions.

Transitions serve two purposes. First, they glue the story together, so it coheres. Second, they form a sequence of bridges to lead you from quote to description to anecdote to background material without tripping over the junctures between ideas or information. The tighter a story, the better the transitions. The more complex a story, the greater the challenge to propel it along with strong, forceful transitions.

These two functions—to unify the feature, yet at the same time to move it in a new direction—gird the story. They provide the underlying shape, the skeleton upon which the flesh of the story hangs. Sometimes writers use the term "architectonics"—which usually refers to the composition of music—to describe this. Architectonics is the structural design that "gives order, balance, and unity to a work, the element of form that relates the parts to each other and to the whole."[1]

Author Richard Rhodes explains:

> The kind of architectonic structures that you have to build, that nobody ever teaches or talks about, are crucial to writing and have little to do with verbal abilities. They have to do with pattern ability and administrative abilities—generalship, if you will. Writers don't talk about it much, unfortunately.

This ability to take command of a feature, to mold it and discipline it and coax the best performance out of each sentence, involves an act of aggression against words. You must control them and not let them control you. It takes time, patience, determination, and experience to get your words to cooperate. But the longer you work at it, the more skilled you will become. As George Orwell warns, "In prose, the worst thing one can do with words is to surrender to them."

Beginning writers too often wait for inspiration, when they should be sweating over little things like transitions. Failure to discipline transitions is one reason why a feature with good potential may seem muddy. Fortunately, good editing can salvage a story that is suffering transition malnutrition. But the task is best done by the author.

Transitions should be short and unobtrusive. Usually, but not always, they are contained in subordinate clauses at the beginning of the first sentence of the paragraph, like trailblazers marking the way. A good way to test the effectiveness of your transitions is to read the first sentence of each paragraph of your story. From them alone, you should be able to tell where you are going, and where you have been.

As with leads, transitions come in many shapes and sizes. However, most transitions fall within one of seven categories:

1. Time
2. Place
3. Mood Changers
4. Repetition
5. Emphatics
6. Pings
7. Quotes

Time

Common time transitions include: next, finally, at last, once, before, now, sometimes, often, today, yesterday, tomorrow (next week, year, etc.), meanwhile, then, until, after, at present, later. Or you can use a day of the week, a season, a date, an hour, a year, or any variation on these.

EXAMPLES:

Sometimes, the people come in wanting autographs.

It happened *on that summer day eighteen months ago.*

A decade ago, breast cancer struck one in thirteen women.

Welzant, in his wrinkled prison clothing at court *last Monday,* seemed an unlikely murderer.

Meanwhile, word of the tragedy spread like wood smoke over this western Missouri town of 2,800.

Place

Place transitions can be general: nearby, down the road, back at the ranch. Or they can be specific, using the name of a town, street, store, or any place that adds local color to the piece. They can also include measurements, from millimeters to kilometers to light years. Place transitions are usually contained within prepositional phrases (a preposition followed by a noun or pronoun).

EXAMPLES:

Up ahead, the Snake River spooled around a long, grassy bend and then out of sight.

Down the hall, a cough rattles, someone moans, a hair dryer comes on.

In the middle of the next cornfield, a solitary streetlight glowed defiantly, a rebel flag tied to its pole.

Anh Duy Nguyen sat *in the office* and talked of bankruptcy.

At Boone, Ames, Marshalltown, Cedar Rapids, at Clinton, hundreds of people gather to cheer the train on.

At a buffet luncheon, he holds court from a folding chair.

Mood Changers[2]

These kinds of transitions help the reader shift psychic gears. They may modify expectations or emotions and may signal what is to come. They may limit, expand upon, deepen, soften, or justify an idea or an action. Many conjunctions or adverbs are valuable mood changers. Common mood changers include: not only/but also, instead, and, so, actually, despite, because, if/then, on the one hand/other hand, besides, but, however, although (even though), as (just as), too, indeed, of course, still, yet, while, in addition to. The use of mood changers helps the writer present the complexities of a person or situation in a brief space.

EXAMPLES:

Yet there is another side to the story.

If tobacco is in its twilight, *then* it had a long time in the sun.

But they still rush from their parents to touch the hand of Mickey Mouse.

And the police simply tried to hold their ground and keep the violence from escalating.

Because blacks and whites work together on the construction projects, the program is a tool for developing racial harmony.

On the other hand, Joe isn't all that impressed with the men of his generation, either.

Despite such assurances, residents say they will continue their opposition.

Not only did Mr. Greenwood invent earmuffs, *he also* designed the machines to mass-produce them.

Repetition

The general rule of thumb for transitions is: the briefer, the better. The transition should be innocuous, not intrusive. And sometimes the most effective way to move the story forward is simply to repeat a key phrase—usually a proper noun or pronoun—from time to time. A single word or phrase may be repeated, or the repetition may consist of varied but related words. This is especially useful in profiles.

In long features that contain lots of description, information, and quotes, the repetition of a person's name as a transition may not be at all noticeable, and may be enough to lubricate the story and keep it running smoothly.

EXAMPLE 1:

A Detroit paper, for instance, profiled a woman, Jean Kline, who died of heroin, and the twin sister, Beth, who survived her. The names of the sisters or other personal references to them are repeated over and over as transitions from one paragraph to the next; yet the reader doesn't notice why this feature is so easy to read. You can, in fact, get a good idea of what the story is about by reading only the first sentences of each paragraph—a sign that the feature is well constructed.

Jean Kline was a child of the working class . . .

Jean and Beth were fraternal twins . . .

The physical likenesses formed a bond between *Jean and Beth.*

Jean was adventurous, a tomboy given to taking dares.

Walter bought *Jean* a bow for their hunting expeditions.

Jean's taste for adventure took other forms.

Beth excelled in her studies . . .

The twins moved in different circles.

In both girls' circles, drugs were easily obtained.

And heroin was "over the line," *Beth* said.

Graduating from high school in 1969, *both girls* found jobs.

She returned to her mother's house in October 1973 for the birth of *Beth's* first child.

And, by the start of the new year, *Jean* had gone over the line.

Years later, *Jean* would tell her friends about her introduction to heroin.

"You'll never understand," *Jean* told Johnson. "There's nothing like it."[3]

The beauty of being able to use repetition for transitions is that it keeps the story "clean" by reducing the volume of words that might otherwise be needed to help propel it along.

Repetition need not be confined to nouns or proper nouns. Any carefully chosen word will do—but be careful. It is more common for writers to repeat words through neglect rather than through a deliberate plan to enhance the story.

However, well-planned repetition—of words or sentence structure—is a traditional rhetorical device and handy literary tool.

EXAMPLE 2:

Here is a feature on a family doctor who has just retired. The author speculates on why this physician—Dr. Rod Buie of Greensboro, North Carolina—is so beloved by his community. She emphasizes the answers with the repetition of sentence structure—in this case, a subordinating conjunction. Notice, too, that these are all sentence *fragments,* which also helps to set them apart from the rest of the story.

Because when Wake Forest scores a touchdown, he marches around the living room singing the Deacons fight song.

Because it never occurred to him to remove the photographs of his childrens' old flames from his office walls.

Because he has told the story of his father getting rheumatic fever in the trenches during World War I so many times that his family can repeat each word and each pause for effect, and it still sounds dramatic to him.

Because he doesn't know how to say no to a call for help or to give up on anything or anyone who has earned his loyalty.

Because no matter what his friends and family do or don't do or say or don't say, it's all right with him.

Because he believed in his work and remained true to the principles on which it was founded.[4]

Emphatics

Emphatics offer an alternative to repeating the same word over and over. They are transitions that nail down the previous thought. Emphatics include: this, that, there, those, these, it, in fact, to say the least, such. These are often adjectives or pronouns, depending on their use in the sentence.

EXAMPLES:

Such a catalyst came in the recent "brotherhood marches" in all-white Forsyth County.

Millions of pounds of *these* chemicals have reached the ground water in many ways.

It is not the kind of attitude Parisians like much.

That saddens 67-year-old Clyde Smith, who's cut hair for 53 years.

Pings

By adding "-ing" to a verb, you create what is called a verbal. These often look like verbs, but act like nouns (called gerunds) or adjectives (called participles). They make wonderful transitions, because the forward momentum set up by a verbal seems to swing the reader ahead into the sentence.

EXAMPLES OF VERB NOUNS:

Designing France's first nuclear bomb shelters was a problem. ["Designing" is the noun; "was" is the verb.]

Stealing power isn't easy. ["Stealing" is the noun; "isn't" is the verb.]

EXAMPLES OF VERB ADJECTIVES:

Wearing high boots and *carrying* long poles and burlap bags, law enforcement officers invaded homes, shops, and offices in Arizona and eight other states earlier this month. ["Wearing" and "carrying" are present participle forms of the verbs "wear" and "carry" and function here as adjectives, modifying the noun "officers"; "invaded" is the verb.]

Sitting in a steel hospital chair, his forehead scarred, the bandages and tubes still clinging to his skin, Darr talked of dealing with his grief. ["Sitting" is the present participle form of the verb "sit" and functions here as an adjective, modifying the noun "Darr"; "talked" is the verb.]

In each of these examples, the reader must reach far into the sentence before finding out what the sentence is about. This helps propel the reader into the subsequent sentence.

But beware. The present participle verb form can also be dangerous because it tends to get entangled in thickets of prose. When using any "-ing" form of the verb, watch your antecedents and your implications. Avoid the ridiculous, such as *"Nailing* down the tent, the dog followed him inside." (This says the dog nailed down the tent. It is called a dangling participle.) Avoid the improbable, such as this published report: "Federal officials learned that the 10,000 employees at a government office building in lower Manhattan were drinking potentially unsafe water at least one month before *informing* anyone, Federal documents show." (This implies that 10,000 government employees conspired to hide the fact they were drinking polluted water.)

When used carefully, however, the present participle is a good transition, giving readers that little extra tug into the story.

Quotes

There are several advantages to leading into a new paragraph, and a new idea, with a quote. It forms a natural watershed from one thought to the next. It adds another perspective. It provides information and insight. It expresses a view (which may or may not agree with the view of the author) and it evokes a response. One of its strongest advantages as a transition is that the quote uses no extra words. But make sure it's not just a weak fill-in. Use only solid, valuable quotes that can stand on their own. (Even when used as a transition, the quote should always serve other purposes as well. See chapter 5, "Quotes.")

EXAMPLES:

A feature on male prostitution in Atlanta addresses the high risk of AIDS among male hustlers. Then it moves to the concerns of police officers on the beat, beginning with a quote by one who fears being attacked with an AIDS-infected syringe.

> "This out here is by far the most dangerous beat in the city," said one officer, nodding toward Sixth and Cypress Streets. "The only one where you can get killed and not know it."[5]

A profile of former Ohio governor and U.S. senator Harold Hughes begins with laudatory reminiscences of his political past. Then it uses a quote as a transition to his current public service.

> "Hello. I'm Harold, and I'm an alcoholic," he said as he stepped to the front of the room at the Jonah Institute to speak to a gathering of alcoholics and the staff at the institute. "We are the lepers of modern America," Hughes told the group.[6]

Each of these two quotes stands on its own; each is personal and insightful. Each also happens to be useful as a transition. Whatever transitions you choose, keep them simple and unobtrusive. But keep them *in;* without them, your reader will be lost.

❏ TRANSITION EXERCISES

1. Clip from a newspaper or magazine a long feature (2,000 words or more) that you found interesting and lively, and read to the very end. Be sure it is nonfiction (not fiction or essay).

- Circle all the transitions used to move the story along.
- Identify each kind of transition.
- Analyze why the writer used these particular transitions.
- Identify paragraphs in which more effective transitions could have been used.

2. Take from your own files your most recent nonfiction writing. It could be a term paper, an essay, or a newspaper or magazine feature (published or unpublished).

- Circle your transitions.
- Identify each kind.
- Notice where you have wordy transitions, and reduce them to under four words where possible.
- Notice where you have inappropriate transitions, and change them.
- Notice where you have no transitions, and insert them if needed.

You may find as you work on transitions that you will want to reorganize parts of your story. It means you are tightening and refining your work; you are editing yourself.

□ **3** □

VERBS

Please do not annoy, torment, pester, plague, molest, worry, badger, harry, harass, heckle, persecute, irk, bullyrag, vex, disquiet, grate, beset, bother, tease, nettle, tantalize, or ruffle the animals.
—THE SAN DIEGO ZOO

English is blessed with great verbs, as some lover of animals and words acknowledged in the above sign. Several commandments govern verb use in feature writing:

1. Never use weak verbs when strong ones will do.
2. Never use one passive voice when the active one will do.
3. Never use the past tense when the present tense will do.
4. Never use big or awkward verbs when little ones will do.
5. Never use adverbs to shore up weak verbs.
6. Never carelessly switch verb tenses.
7. Never violate subject-verb agreement.

Let's look at these rules and, equally important, their exceptions. (And then we'll discuss the bane of all writers, the pronoun.)

Never Use Weak Verbs
When Strong Ones Will Do

Verbs can make or break a story. And nothing will break a story faster than a string of listless verbs. The main culprits are forms of the verbs *to be, to go, to do, to get, to have, to make.* There is nothing wrong with these verbs per se. Far from it. They are a staple of our language. They are comfortable and familiar; they don't startle or disconcert. But too many, thrown around carelessly, will make readers feel like they are slogging through quicksand; when the drag becomes great enough, readers balk and stop—which is fair enough. After all, if the writer has not been patient enough to sow the story with hardy verbs, then why should the reader muster enough patience to slog on?

Verb abuse is a sign that the writer may in fact be sloppy about word choice in general, so that the sentences suffer not only from verbal anemia but also from other kinds of neglect. The same writers tend to lean on vagueness and clichés, so that the story slowly sinks, unloved and untended, into the tepid purgatory where all such syntax deserves to go.

Whenever you feel stuck for a pithy verb, consult a thesaurus. It doesn't always give you what you want, but it does prod the brain.

Strong verbs tend to be particularly important in sentences that contain description. This is because description, while crucial to the life of a story, also stops the forward progress of the story to focus on specific details that will give it depth and breadth. To overcome this slowed momentum, it is useful, whenever possible, to *wrap* description around action verbs to keep the story moving.

Here is an example of a stalled description:

> She *is* small and frail and *wears* a tattered red dress.
>
> She *goes* over to the child, *bends* down, and *picks* him up.

The problem here is that the first sentence contains all description, and no action. The second sentence plods along behind with weak verbs. To correct this, it can be rewritten:

> The tattered dress *clings to* (or *shifts loosely on*) her frail body as she *bends* to *pick up* the child.

In this edit, three weak verbs are cut: is, wears, goes. They are replaced with one new verb—clings—which describes a more graphic *action*. By folding the description from the first sentence into the action of the second sentence, the story no longer stalls. Instead, the description becomes an unobtrusive part of the action.

Verbs are a powerful tool when used to enhance an already dramatic scene. A few years ago, when a teenager killed her parents in Milburnton, Tennessee, the reporter recreated the terror with careful description wrapped around riveting verbs.

> The first bullet *hit* Jean Turnmire in the left breast.
>
> "Ginger, I love you," the woman said as her 15-year-old daughter *squeezed* the trigger again.
>
> The second shot *struck* the left side of the woman's head, *killing* her instantly and making the third bullet, which *slammed* into her back as she *slumped* forward on her bed, unnecessary.
>
> J. S. Turnmire, *hearing* the gunshots in the back of the house, *leaped* from his easy chair in the den and *began running* towards his wife's bedroom.
>
> He *made* it to the hallway.

There, a single bullet *hit* him in the left nostril, *ripping* apart the lower half of his brain.[1]

This brutal scene becomes even more unforgettable when described with the arsenal of verbs: hit, squeeze, strike, kill, slam, slump, leap, run, rip. It would have been less awful if the reporter had simply written a straight news story: "According to testimony, Mrs. Turnmire *was shot* three times. Her husband *was shot* once while trying to come to her aid."

Instead, the re-creation of the gruesome moment with the compelling verbs that heighten the massacre make this an unforgettable scene—as much as one might like to forget it.

But it is the undramatic moments—the ho-hum scenarios of everyday life—that provide the real challenge in verb use. Then the writer's ingenuity is put to the test. Trying to insert verve into a political luncheon, a public-relations event, a grand opening or ground-breaking; trying to spice up the profile of a person who is uncooperative or boring—these are the features in which writers must pry out those verbs that may salvage the story.

Indeed, verbs can save the writer who is faced with the formidable task of trying to make people and events look more interesting than they really are.

Here is how one reporter handled a public-relations birthday party for singer Jerry Lee Lewis, held at a bar in Memphis, Tennessee.

> Invitations in hand, his friends *surged* into Hernando's Hideaway, a wood-paneled juke joint on Memphis' south side, to *get liquored up* and to *party* all night long last Monday . . .
> *Squeezing* around his table, they *jockeyed* for his attention. Big-boned, hulking farmers *vied* with publicity men in leisure suits to *shake* his hand. Bored young women in leather and chiffon *pressed* against giddy middle-aged ladies with beehive hairstyles to *take* snapshots and *peck* him on the cheek.[2]

Every verb is pulling its weight here; every verb carries momentum. Not because the story lends itself to these particular verbs, but because the writer found the verbs and lent them to the story. The less experienced writer might have written it this way:

> Several hundred people *came* to Hernando's Hideaway, a wood-paneled juke joint on Memphis' south side, to *have* a good time and *try to shake* the hand of Jerry Lee Lewis. The people there *ranged from* big-boned hulking farmers to publicity men in leisure suits, from bored young women in leather and chiffon to giddy middle-aged ladies with beehive hairstyles.

This is the kind of prose often produced by beginning writers—a prose not yet sensitive to the power of verbs. The problem in this second example is that all the action occurs in the first sentence; the second sentence contains only description. So the writer has two tasks here: first, to integrate the action and description; second, to beef up the verbs. Why use limp verbs like "have," "try," and "range" when lively verbs like "surge," "liquor up," "party," "jockey," and "vie" are available?

Effective use of verbs depends not only on your mastery of the subtleties of the English language, but also on your perceptiveness in gathering the kinds of description that can be wrapped effectively around the verbs (see chapter 4, "Description"). If you are observant enough, you can insert action in places where, to the untrained eye, no action seems to tread.

Here, for example, is a profile of a train announcer at Pennsylvania Station, a man whose sedentary job it is to sit in a booth all day long and call out train arrivals and departures.

> He *sits* alone in a darkened Plexiglass booth that *juts* from the wall 10 feet above the floor of the main waiting room. One day

this week, a commuter *leaned* against a post and *waited* for Mr. Simmons to *bellow* his next "All aboard!", then *gave* him the thumbs-up sign and *hustled* off to work. An elderly woman *waited* for an "All aboard!", then *blew* Mr. Simmons a kiss and *was* on her way.

Up in the booth, Mr. Simmons *barked* out the last call for The Crescent. An elderly couple *applauded.* A young couple *held* each other in a fast embrace. A young man *crashed* through the crowd, *racing* for the train, and several commuters *charging* to another train *sang* out the "All aboard!" in chorus with Mr. Simmons.[3]

This job is basically boring, as the subject Daniel Simmons himself pointed out to the writer. So the writer finds ways to compensate. First, he uses strong verbs when describing Simmons's work. His booth doesn't just stick out or protrude from a wall, it assertively *juts* out; Simmons doesn't just announce loudly, he *bellows,* he *barks.*

Second, the writer spices up the story by including others' reactions to Simmons's voice. By focusing on a few moments in a given day, and by watching carefully, the writer is able to capture the kind of detail that lets him incorporate more zest—people lean, hustle, blow, applaud, hold, crash, race, sing—into an essentially quiescent story. Because the writer captures these responses *from* others, rather than relying on Mr. Simmons's response *to* others, the writer has managed to work his way around the story until he finds an "in" for action verbs.

In fact, no matter how quiet a moment, a good writer can capture it with compelling, assertive verbs. Here, for instance, is how one writer described a widow at a memorial service for her husband.

Her head *fell* forward as the bugler began to play, her hair *covered* her face like a curtain, and her face *folded* like paper, and then she *raised* her head, *swung* the hair back, almost defiant in her determination to face up, to be strong.[4]

The untrained eye might see only a woman sitting quietly, a look of grief on her face. This writer notices the small details, and then couples them with a series of verbs that indicate first a closing in upon oneself, a descent into grief—fall, cover, fold—and then a tentative spark of strength, of tenacity, with verbs like "raise" and "swing."

Never Use the Passive Voice When the Active One Will Do

The passive voice carelessly used slows the pace of the story. When verbs are active, so is the sentence. When verbs are passive, the sentence also loses its punch: instead of doing something, the subject has something done *to* it. For example:

> *Active:* She *passed* the potatoes around the table.

> *Passive:* The potatoes *were passed* around the table.

When a sentence is in the passive voice, we don't know *who* is performing the action. The actor is missing, unknown unless a phrase is added.

The impact of the passive voice is to wind the sentence back upon itself, so that instead of moving forward it seems to be elliptical, with the verb guiding the reader backward toward the subject of the sentence rather than onward to the object. This is reflected in the way the passive voice is traditionally diagrammed; the line preceding the verb on the diagram leans forward, toward the subject, like this:

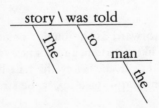

But be forewarned that verbs are feisty creatures, chafing at their barricades. In fact, much of what follows will deal with exceptions to this rule to favor the active voice. Nevertheless, the rule itself stands firm.

There are times, for instance, when the passive verb form is unavoidable, and even acceptable. It occurs often, for instance, when writers describe a legal action: she *was released* on bond; he *was read* his rights; police *were called* to the scene; court *was adjourned;* they *were promised* immunity.

While these sentences could be converted to the active voice (the judge *released* her on bond; the police *read* him his rights; a telephone call *brought* police to the scene; the judge *adjourned* the court; the district attorney *promised* immunity) the change doesn't improve the copy, and can even seem awkward. Common usage wins out.

The passive voice also might be used when the subject is an unknown or amorphous "other"—whether an individual or a group. For example:

The toxic wastes *had been put* on his property about 20 years ago.

Many solutions to save the Acropolis *have been offered.*

In emergencies, planes *are chartered* to save lives.

The government's plan to demolish the camp by the end of the year *has been deferred* for the time being.

It is understood in the above sentences that the strength of the sentence lies not in who performed the action, but in the potential *results* of the action—dumping toxic wastes, saving the Acropolis, chartering planes, deferring the demolition.

The passive voice is also a way to avoid inserting the reporter into the story when the reporter is a witness to an event or a conversation:

From his office window, overlooking barbed-wire fences and barren ground, a convoy of white soldiers *could be seen* patrolling Soweto.

Here, the reporter is the one who observed the military patrol during an interview. The use of the passive voice is a way to convey this information without using the pronoun "I," or the equally awkward "one," or "a reporter," as in "a reporter saw a convoy of white soldiers . . ."

Or, consider this profile of a judge who has come under attack for never voting to affirm a death penalty verdict.

> The chief justice of the California Supreme Court *is asked* to imagine, momentarily, that she is gazing across her desk at the mother of a murdered child.

This is a key question in this interview, a chance for the writer to play devil's advocate. However, it would be intrusive for the reporter to write "I asked the chief justice of the California Supreme Court to imagine. . . ." It would detract from the real subject of the story—the judge and her opinions. The passive voice is a neutral shield to keep the writer from intruding upon the reader.

If you are really confident about your ability to control a story through verb use, the passive voice may also be used from time to time as a literary device to reflect a person's helplessness or inability to control a situation. One example is in this story about an elderly couple being harassed by teenagers:

> On a night around Easter, his house *was bombarded* with raw eggs.

Or in this story of a fatal accident about to happen during the filming of a movie:

> Behind them things *were blowing up,* brilliant, thudding, high cascades of light.

Each of these sentences has other strengths to compensate for the passive verb form. First, the verbs themselves are lively: "bombard" and "blow up." Second, the construction (or architectonics) of the sentences compensates for the passive voice.

Let's look at the first sentence. It both begins ("On a night around Easter") and ends ("with raw eggs") with prepositional phrases that together absorb the weight of the sentence. The emphasis is at the beginning and the end, and the verb—the hostile action—acts like a hinge around which the sentence swings.

In the second sentence, the tension seems to rise slowly to a crescendo in the series of descriptions *beyond* the verb— "brilliant, thudding, high cascades of light." This combination of passive verb and delayed action makes the sentence seem to move in suspenseful slow motion—there is violence, but as seen from a distance, like a far-off bombing.

Or, you can deliberately use the passive voice to break out of a string of active verbs in order to alter the pace of the story. When you use passive verbs in this way, they also tend to highlight information that precedes or follows.

Here, for example, is how two writers describe U.S. Customs Service agents tracking a drug-laden plane as it returns from Colombia, South America, to Florida.

> Radios *began to buzz* as voices *detail* the northward path of the plane. Agents *scramble* to *open* metal lockers and *pass out* flight bags. Pistols *are strapped* on belt loops. Handguns *are slipped* into shoulder holsters and boots. Shotguns *are filled* with shells.
>
> Pilots *huddle* over a maze of maps which *cover* the long route from Florida to an isolated, unlit airfield deep in the Pocono Mountains of Pennsylvania, where the target plane *is expected to land.*
>
> Bullet-proof vests *are handed out.* Half-smoked cigarettes *are crushed* into overflowing ashtrays. The agents *rush* out the door to their waiting planes.[5]

Out of the sixteen verbs used, more than one-third are passive. Yet the scene seems to crackle with action. Why?

First, the verbs are small but powerful, and all but the first one ("began") are in the present tense: buzz, scramble, strap, slip, huddle, cover, crush, rush.

The writer is also careful to bracket the entire scene with active verbs: the first two sentences and the last sentence are in the active, not the passive, voice (and have peppy verbs like buzz, scramble, rush). And notice how the passive verbs, with one exception, are confined to short, brisk sentences. That exception comes in the long single sentence in the middle paragraph, which helps to break up the repetitiveness of the short, snappy sentences in the first and third paragraphs. That long sentence also helps emphasize the action-packed shorter ones around it.

It is unlikely, of course, that the writers sat down and did a content analysis of the impact of using the passive voice in this scene. Rather, they had a sense of what "works" in their copy—an intuition about language that comes only with careful attention to word choice and syntax, and that improves with experience.

Consider how their story would flow if they had followed a hard-and-fast rule of using active voice only:

> Radios began to buzz as voices detail the northward path of the plane. Agents scramble to open metal lockers and pass out flight bags. They strap pistols on belt loops. They fill shotguns with shells.
>
> Pilots huddle over a maze of maps which cover the long route from Florida to an isolated, unlit airfield deep in the Pocono Mountains of Pennsylvania, where they expect the target plane to land.
>
> The supervisor hands out bullet-proof vests. Agents crush half-smoked cigarettes into overflowing ashtrays. They rush out the door to their waiting planes.

Not bad. It would pass most editors' desks. But the lack of variety in the verbs makes this less snappy than the original.

However, keep in mind that the above exceptions prove the rule. Only use the passive voice with intent—to produce a certain effect—and always use it with care.

When possible, stick to the active voice. It will get you there faster.

Never Use the Past Tense When the Present Tense Will Do

Writing in the present makes the story seem more immediate, as in the above example. Use it whenever possible. It particularly lends itself to profiles or "offbeat" features about places, people, or situations. If you do a feature on a local bakery, a profile of a fire chief, or an in-depth report of a controversy over an abortion clinic, it can be presented in the present tense as long as the bakery, fire chief, and controversy remain extant.

Never Use Big or Awkward Verbs When Little Ones Will Do

Big verbs come in several disguises. There are pretentious ones, silly ones, bloated ones. In general, the bigger the verb the more oblique its meaning. Short verbs tend to be more concise.

As the language evolves, adjectives and nouns are sometimes made into verbs, such as "to network," "to finalize," "to fault," "to bus," "to hassle." These verbs seem jarring when they first appear.

A recently heard one is "to office," as in "She is not officing today" (meaning she is not coming in to work). Another of recent vintage is "to dorm," as in "John and I dorm together."

Computer literature is producing an interesting and

sometimes irresistible array of new verbs, as "to bibble" (search through a bibliography).[6] Presumably, one could say: "I am going to bibble around in my computer." Or perhaps: "Please bibble my database."

The words "and" and "or," known by most of us as conjunctions, have also been transformed into computer verbs. To "and" something means you are going to ask your computer to search for a listing of a group of topics such as: "Australia *and* Kangaroos." To "or" something means you are going to ask your computer to search for a group of alternative topics or phrases, such as "Australia *or* Kangaroos." This is known in computer lingo as a "hedge," and is used most often if you are unsure about the terms used in a database. So don't be surprised if some day your local librarian explains: "You can *or* these terms and then *and* them with the topic of interest."[7]

Because language is malleable, and always in a state of flux, it is hard to know which of these "new" verbs will eventually enter mainstream English, and which will just fade away. H. L. Mencken complained way back in 1919 about many new verbs-from-nouns, such as "to contact," "to audition," "to curb," "to alert," "to package," "to research," "to panic," and "to option"—all of which are now standard linguistic fare. Mencken, who listed many that never made it to the end of the century ("to music," "to biography," "to siesta," "to guest"), also had this to say about verbs and their relatives:

> The nouns in common use, in the main, are quite sound in form. The adjectives, too, are treated rather politely, and the adverbs, though commonly transformed into the forms of their corresponding adjectives, are not further mutilated. But the verbs and pronouns undergo changes which set off the common speech very sharply from both correct English and correct American. This is only natural, for it is among the verbs and

pronouns that nearly all the remaining inflections in English are to be found, and so they must bear the chief pressure of the influences that have been warring upon every sort of inflection since the earliest days.[8]

But if you are thinking of being creative and cute with verbs, a good rule to follow is: proceed with caution. An out-of-place noun or adjective used as a verb will probably detract from the larger story at hand. It is better to master the compendium of existing verbs before you start creating new ones. Read John McPhee (who cultivates verbs like "to parse," "to sein") to get a sense of the big ideas that can come from small verbs. Keep it short. Keep it simple. Keep it moving.

Never Use Adverbs to Shore Up Weak Verbs (Use a Stronger Verb Instead)

Avoid phrases like "speak softly" (just use whisper) or "move swiftly" (just use run, jog, trot, or dash).

Writers unaware of the power of verbs tend to use adverbs where none are needed. In most cases, a strong verb is strong enough on its own; the adverb is redundant. A few from recently published stories include:

wander away	wander
totally destroy	destroy
seriously consider	consider
wink slyly	wink
be absolutely sure	be sure
be definitely interested	be interested
be perfectly clear	be clear
search frantically	search
mercilessly tortured	tortured

Use adverbs only when they add a descriptive ingredient to the story that a verb cannot supply:

> He *viciously* attacked with a sharp chisel a three-ton block of limestone. [He could have attacked it hesitantly, skillfully, etc.]

> Peter Mpumelelo paced *disconsolately* in the sand. [He could have paced thoughtfully, eagerly, etc.]

Never Carelessly Switch Verb Tenses

Ground your story in one tense. If you start your story in the present tense, stay there. If you start in the past tense, stay there. You can then use other tenses as needed to indicate corollary time changes in the story. Many beginning writers inadvertently change tenses in a feature. It is confusing for the reader, and will be caught by an editor (one hopes) before it goes to print. But editors slip up too. The ultimate responsibility for producing clean, clear, readable prose rests with the writer. If you frustrate and confuse your readers with inconsistent verb tenses, they will avenge themselves by turning to another story.

Never Violate Subject-Verb Agreement

Single subjects take single verbs; plural subjects take plural verbs. Once verbs start to wander from the vicinity of the subject, mistakes appear. Take this story from the *International Herald Tribune:*

> The very *visibility* that makes Mrs. Gorbachev the object of approving and consuming curiosity in the West *have* led to a broad feeling in many levels of Soviet society that she is somehow overstepping her position. [It should be: visibility *has.*]

Or this one from the *New York Times:*

The official radio said his *resignation* from the leadership of
both the Burmese Government and the ruling party *were* accepted. [It should be: *was* accepted.]

These basic errors made it past some of the world's best
editors.

One way to check on how well you are abiding by the
seven verb rules in the chapter is to go through your own story
when you are done writing, and highlight your verbs. You
will then be able to see if you have too many dull, passive, or
overblown verbs, verbs shored up by superfluous adverbs, or
errors in verb tense or agreement.

Verbs *alone* do not make or break a story, of course. It
is, in fact, possible at least in theory to write a Pulitzer Prize–
winning feature using only dull, passive verbs. Verbs are but
one component—albeit an important one—in the complex,
subtle, sophisticated machinery that constitutes a sentence, a
paragraph, or a page of prose.

But inattention to verbs usually indicates a general laxity
about language. Only strong nouns, and a good sense of the
heft of a sentence—how it will handle itself on the page—will
compensate for shaky verbs.

Never Give In to Pronoun Misuse

I would like to add a word here about another common cause
of grammatical glitches—the pronoun. Writers need to be
sure that the pronoun agrees with its antecedent. Every pronoun has an antecedent—a noun to which the pronoun refers. Your task is to be sure that if the antecedent is *singular,*
then the pronoun is *singular* as well. For example: "The
doctor **claims** her diagnosis is correct." Since the antecedent "doctor" is singular, then the pronoun "her" is also

singular. If the antecedent is plural, then the pronoun must also be plural, as in: "The doctors **claim** their diagnoses are correct." This is not always as easy as it sounds, however.

The farther away the pronoun drifts from its antecedent, the greater the risk of error. This is especially true when other nouns intervene between the pronoun and antecedent. As in: "The doctors, after meeting with the lawyers, claim the diagnoses are correct and stand by their opinion. They know they must defend them if their doubts persist."

Who knows who must defend whom (or what) if whose doubts persist? This kind of muddle quickly leads to reader burnout. Few readers will attempt to untangle the pronouns and nouns—nor should they. It is the responsibility of the writer to do so. It would save confusion by simply rewriting it: "After seeking legal advice, the doctors know they must defend their diagnoses should doubts persist."

As linguist Jacques Barzun writes, pronouns inhabit a "dangerous wilderness. It is the duty of pronouns to be not wild but tamed, that is, tied down; yet their natural tendency is toward the jungle."

In addition, because of the rules of English, some singular personal pronouns ("he/she," "him/her," "his/hers") lead to intrinsic sexism if not used with care. This problem exists in part because English lacks a unisex singular pronoun in the third person such as the French "on." Our closest equivalent, "one," has a stilted quality to it that makes it an unacceptable substitute for "he" and "she." As a result, we commonly read inappropriately gender-specific writing even by sensitive grammarians who should know better. William Zinsser, for instance, insists on retaining the male pronoun even when including women in general statements. In his advice to beginning writers, he points out:

> If a *reader is* lost, it is generally because the writer has not been careful enough to keep *him* on the path.[9]

This sentence is grammatically correct. The subject, verb, and personal pronoun are singular. But if the subject, "a reader," means "the average reader," or "the typical reader"—male or female—then the sentence is logically incorrect. The subject is non-sex-specific, while the pronoun is sex-specific. And let us assume Zinsser did not intend to imply that the only readers who get lost are male readers. To correct the sexism, here are four possible solutions.

1. The sentence could say:

> If *readers* are lost, it is generally because the writer has not been careful enough to keep *them* on the path.

While this is now grammatically and syntactically correct, it loses some of its punch to transform the example of one reader into all readers. A specific example is always better than a general one.

2. Or, the sentence could say:

> If a *reader* is lost, it is generally because the writer has not been careful enough to keep *him* or *her* on the path.

This, too, is correct in its grammar and syntax, but the reader stumbles slightly over the double pronouns "him or her" near the end.

3. Another commonly used, though technically incorrect, option is:

> If a *reader* is lost, it is generally because the writer has not been careful enough to keep *them* on the path.

The sentence is now grammatically a mess since the plural pronoun is referring to a singular antecedent.

4. The final option is to recast the sentence:

> If a *reader* is lost, it is generally because the writer has not been careful enough *to clear the path.*

This gets rid of the pronoun, and the problem, though it involves more effort and thought in the rewriting. Unfortunately, it also slightly changes the meaning of the sentence. (To clear the path, and to keep someone on the path, imply different skills in path-making.) But when it comes to clarity of language—whether grammatical or syntactical—it seems to provide the least jarring solution.[10]

But more people are beginning to accept the third option above as an acceptable solution: using a plural pronoun with a singular antecedent. Even the linguistic purist Mencken seemed to condone it by quoting several examples from presidents and judges who have used it in this century: "No *man* or *woman* can hesitate to give what *they* have"; "*Someone* told me last night that *they . . .*"; "We should keep it possible for *anyone* to correct *their* errors"; and "No *person* can be happy in life if *they . . .*" Mencken added, "In the lower reaches of the language, the plural is used with complete innocence, and such forms as '*Everybody* knows *their* way', '*Somebody* has gotten *theirs*', '*Nobody* could help *themselves*' . . . are common."[11]

❑ VERB AND PRONOUN EXERCISES

1. Here is a wire service description of a saloon on the edge of the Cheyenne Indian reservation in Jimtown, Montana. Rewrite it to incorporate action verbs with the description.

> The saloon is a battered wooden building bearing vague evidence that it once knew paint. Its windows are screened with steel, of prison thickness. The sign over the door, "Jimtown Bar," is riddled with more than 100 bullet holes. The equally ventilated mailbox is the third replacement in less than a year.
>
> Inside, a bar of raw oak runs the length of the room. In front of it are spaced 16 cottonwood tree trunks, each a foot and a half thick, smoothed by denim and gouged by knives. There

is no other furniture. The bar rail is fastened not to the bar but to the tree trunks. "I couldn't keep stools," Bob Edwards said. "They kept busting them over each other's heads."

2. Clip from your local newspaper a feature that you find particularly bland. It could be about a person, a place, or an event.

- Circle all the verbs.
- How many of them would you classify as "dull" verbs (to be, to go, to do, to get, to have, to make)?
- How many are in the passive voice?
- Rewrite to reduce weak verbs and passive voice.
- Now highlight only the sentences that contain description.
- Rewrite those sentences where necessary, wrapping the description around stronger verbs.

3. Circle all the "dull" verbs in this chapter. (Or this book, for the more energetic.) How many can be replaced with livelier verbs? Rewrite as many of these dull verb sentences as you can.
4. The English language seems to conspire against the non-sexist use of pronouns, but avoiding sexism is possible through diligence and creative rewording. Rewrite this published sentence to avoid sexism in pronoun use.

A restaurant diner would have no way to know whether *he* was eating clams from the North Jersey Shore unless the proprietor knew, and was willing to say, where *his* purchase had originated.

5. The following examples contain one or more errors in agreement of subject-verb, or pronoun-antecedent. Correct as necessary.

A. Is she one of the women who was picketing?
B. Each of the ideas presented in class were valuable.

C. When the *Chicago Tribune* sends correspondents overseas, they often provide help in relocating their families.

D. Has any of the statistics been released?

E. Everyone on the boat knows that he will need to swim to shore.

F. Read Plutarch's *Lives.* They will teach you about leadership.

G. The House of Representatives voted against the bills because they were eager to recess.

H. When a child is cranky, it usually means they are tired.

Figure out your own answers first. Then read the following corrections and comments. Feel free to argue with them. Remember, English is a living, changing, challenging language. Here are explanations for the preceding agreement exercises:[12]

A. Here, the subject of a sentence is singular ("she") and the noun in the prepositional phrase between the subject and verb is plural ("women"). You may have been taught to ignore the prepositional phrase when deciding whether the verb of a sentence should be singular or plural. This rule, however, should not be followed slavishly. In this sentence, the clause "who was picketing" really describes all the "women" and not "she" or "one." The correct sentence is: Is she one of the women who were picketing?

B. The pronoun "each" is usually considered to be singular. But it's always best to look at the meaning of the sentence as well. Here, the writer is conveying the idea that each of the ideas presented in class is being considered one by one, and each *one* is valuable. The correct sentence is: Each of the ideas presented in class was valuable.

C. The *Chicago Tribune* employs many people, but the paper itself is a single institution. So while it may sound awkward colloquially, "it" is the proper pronoun. Using "it" also avoids the ambiguity of whether "they" refers to the newspaper or to the correspondents. The correct sentence is: When the *Chicago Tribune* sends correspondents overseas, it often provides help in relocating their families.

D. Again, look at what you are trying to say to the reader. If this is a situation where one statistic might be released, reword the sentence: Has any statistic been released? But if you are describing a case where some statistics (perhaps as few as one but probably more) might be released, then the plural verb is correct: Have any of the statistics been released?

E. The grammatical rule that the pronoun "he" must be used following indefinite pronouns is no longer absolute. Linguistic studies have shown that "he" used in this so-called generic way does not reflect how men and women actually think when they use the pronoun. Possible alternatives to the false generic "he" are "he or she," or even "they," in some cases. But before automatically substituting one of these choices ("he or she" seems awkward to many, and in this sentence "he and she" is more accurate), first see whether the sentence can be reworded. This sentence could read: All on the boat know they will need to swim to shore.

F. *Lives* may be a plural word but it refers to only one book: It will teach you about leadership.

G. The House of Representatives is, like the *Chicago Tribune*, a single institution but it's awkward to think of an institution as being "eager." Rather than automatically changing "they" to "it," however, it might make more sense to change "they" to a plural noun. A possibility: The House of Representatives voted against the bills because the members were eager to recess.

H. Here, it isn't just some particular child who is cranky when tired. Your telling the reader that fatigue makes most children cranky. So change the singular in the first clause to a plural, and the rest follows naturally: When children are cranky, it usually means they are tired.

□4□
DESCRIPTION

DESCRIPTION IS THE LIFEBLOOD of the feature story. As Ernest Hemingway put it, "Experience is communicated by these small details, intimately preserved, which have the effect of indicating the whole." Three steps are needed to produce good description: first, gathering it; second, choosing how much of it to put in the story; third, deciding where to put it.

Most beginning writers need to work diligently on the first step—gathering description. No matter how brilliant their comprehension of the nuances of language, their copy often seems flat because they have failed to observe enough detail *at the scene.* As a result, they lack "color" for their feature.

Train Yourself to Observe

When gathering description, try to view the world without predilection. Put aside any biases that may distort what you see or impair your objectivity in the way you see it. Train yourself to notice *every* detail, like a painter; your palette is the paper upon which you will paint a word picture. Later, when you paint, you may choose to emphasize the warts, or glamorize the mundane. But as you collect information, withhold judgment, so that everything remains fresh and full of possibility. None of us can mentally record the barrage of sights, sounds, and smells that accost us all the time; there's simply too much to absorb. But we can train ourselves to notice these details while "on the job." Stephen Spender once said of fellow poet W. B. Yeats that

> he went for days on end without noticing anything, but then, about once a month, he would look out of a window and suddenly be aware of a swan or something and it gave him such a stunning shock that he'd write a marvelous poem about it.[1]

That intensity of awareness, that ability to look at the familiar and *see* it as if for the first time, sets not only the great poet but also the great reporter apart from the merely competent.

Most of the time we look and do not see. But many people drawn to writing sense from childhood that they have a special ability to observe the world, to capture the moment that others overlook, to see "the edges" of things.

Joan Didion says her attention was always drawn to the concrete rather than to the abstract, and in her writing both as a journalist and a novelist she uses biting imagery to convey her views of modern culture.

In college, she recalls:

> My attention veered inexorably back to the specific, to the tangible, to what was generally considered, by everyone I knew then and for that matter have known since, the peripheral. I would try to contemplate the Hegelian dialectic and would find myself concentrating instead on a flowering pear

tree outside my window and the particular way the petals fell on my floor. I would try to read linguistic theory and would find myself wondering instead if the lights were on in the bevatron up the hill. . . . I can no longer tell you whether Milton put the sun or the earth at the center of his universe in "Paradise Lost," the central question of at least one century and a topic about which I wrote 10,000 words that summer, but I can still recall the exact rancidity of the butter in the City of San Francisco's dining car, and the way the tinted windows on the Greyhound bus cast the oil refineries around Carquinez Straits into a grayed and obscurely sinister light. In short, my attention was always on the periphery . . ."[2]

In fact, the "best" journalist has a poet's instinct for minute details. In this sense, the demands imposed on writers of nonfiction—the need to be specific, to use the concrete to trigger an intangible but powerful response—are similar to the demands imposed on poets and novelists.

At the start of each new feature writing class, I often read a poem laden with specific imagery and then ask students to free associate from the poem and to make a list that reduces feelings evoked by the poem into one vivid word or phrase. Typical examples of their efforts:

200-year-old trees twisting towards the passing autumn
a blind eagle falling in spirals from the sky
a blind retreating

Another wrote:

the spiritual sanctum of a TV Buddha created by a pr flak
bubble-gum popping teenagers in clogs, Calvins, and Farrah
Fawcett hairdos talk about true love

A third wrote:

birds newborn in a nest
an empty house sparsely furnished

white curtains flying
people kneeling on a knoll praying
old men lonely and afraid
white beards, very long
blinding light then clouds
no sound then chirp of baby birds

What does this have to do with journalism? Or with facts? For a start, it is specific. It is an attempt to order description that will evoke emotion, convey innuendo, imply the imminence of revelation. Feature prose that packs a wallop demands this kind of poetic sensibility. It demands the concrete. It demands brevity that comes from selection, not compression. It demands an awareness that what is left out is as important as what is put in.

In fact, some of the best journalistic description you read in newspapers or magazines is sometimes just a carefully constructed list. Here is how one writer described the experience of a Maryland family who was being harassed by local teenagers.

BB pellets, slingshots, broken windows, a burning shoe, stolen trash cans, uprooted wooden flower planters, broken aerials, foreign cars hefted onto lawns, trash fires, tossed raw eggs, broken beer bottles, curses, loud radios, loitering, trees set on fire, fights. And snowballs. Every winter, snowballs.[3]

And here is the lead for a profile of Mary Lou Retton, the first American woman to win an Olympic gold medal in gymnastics.

Black stirrup pants. Rhinestone bracelets. Madonna-esque earrings. Red nail polish. She is the archetypal teenage girl ready for a trip to the mall.

Monumental calves. Granite thighs. Shoulders that will never need padding. The smile. She is Mary Lou, ready for another exhibition of perkiness.[4]

A feature writer's list of images, of course, is constrained by facts, and it is always annoying, not to mention unethical, when writers untether their concrete facts and let them soar into the stratosphere of purple prose. But most beginning writers do not even begin to develop the descriptive possibilities of a story. They miss what Didion calls the "shimmer" around the edges of things. To write a good story, you must note those edges: color, texture, smell, sound, quiet, tone of voice, body language, small things lying around.

Say, for instance, you are doing a feature on an all-night diner. You walk in at midnight. One customer, a man, is sitting alone in the back, eating a sandwich.

What is he wearing? Are his clothes pressed or wrinkled? Frayed or new? What color are his shoes? Are they shiny or scuffed? Do they look like sturdy American-made shoes with thick soles, or fine Italian shoes? What color are his socks? Are they bagging, or do they hug his ankles? What is he eating? Does he eat it fast or slow? How does he hold his fork? Is he a crumb-wiper? A chin-dabber? A dribbler? What is his posture: erect, hunched, legs crossed, ankles crossed, shoulders tilted in one direction? Does he seem self-conscious or relaxed, and what is it about the way he sits and moves that conveys this impression? What color is his hair? Thick or thin? Well-cut or shabby? Is he wearing glasses? What color are the frames? What is the quality of the way he looks at other people in the restaurant: curious, furtive, shameful, eager, indifferent? What is it, specifically, that conveys that quality? What is the shape of his lips?

These are a fraction of the questions about this man for which you should have the answers, written in your notes, before you leave the diner. Then you need to turn your attention to the physical description of the diner itself, to the interaction or lack of interaction among people—to the ambiance or "vibes" of the place and its occupants.

A certain feeling comes over writers as they gather this kind of careful description. It is like having radar on the top of your head, slowly circling round and round. While going through this process, most writers feel distanced, disengaged from not only the scene but from themselves: they become objective nonparticipants, storers of information. To be truly present, they become in an immediate sense not present—evanescent, omniscient, passive receptacles of data.

This is why it is very important *not* to report on an event in which you are also a participant. If you are going to write about a ball game, a disco, a march, a beach, don't plan to join in the action and just take a few notes along the way. If you're going to report, then report. If you're going to join, then join. The two don't mix. Experienced feature writers know this; novices usually learn the hard way.

When gathering information, it is also very important to *write down everything.* Later, you can decide what to throw out and what to keep. The tendency, unfortunately, is to think: "Oh, I'll remember that he wore wire-framed bifocals and that his tie was crooked. Besides, I probably won't need that kind of stuff anyway." Then you arrive back at the office or home, begin to write, and find yourself searching for that tiny missing detail to flesh out the story, or to illustrate a point. It's not in your notes, so you try to visualize the scene: *Was* she biting her fingernails just then? *Were* his eyes blue? Now *why* did she seem sinister? You're sure it wasn't your imagination, but how can you prove it to the readers?

Not only have you wasted time looking through your notes for information that is not there, you may have also lost the opportunity to choose that "perfect" detail to illustrate your story.

Consider, for example, the kind of annotated attention this reporter must have paid to Joan Collins during her most recent divorce trial.

> On Wednesday Joan Collins was on the witness stand. It was hard not to fixate on her lips. She has these amazing lips, sort of full and bowed and constantly at work there below the

smoke-colored eyelids and the large tousled hair. The hair was mesmerizing too, especially on Wednesday, when a single velvet bow appeared to be perilously containing the whole arrangement, and when she walked back into the courtroom after lunch she had a peach-colored rose in one hand and the black velvet bow in the back—and she would lift the rose to her face, you see, as though preparing to kiss it—

Anyway, the lips. These lips are worth $95,000 per episode, which is what Collins testified she made last season on "Dynasty." These lips pouted, and pursed, and made small moues in the general direction of the press corps, which was dutifully taking notes.[5]

The mesmerizing, almost obsessive, quality of this description of hair, eyelids, and especially lips captures in a tangible way some of the intangible allure that surrounds this particular superstar. It represents all that was sensual, frivolous, fascinating about this event.

The most difficult things to describe are these intangibles—smells, body language, a certain look in the eye, the sound of a voice. Here, for instance, is a careful description of the pronunciation of two words. It appeared in the feature on the train announcer in Pennsylvania Station (see chapter 3, "Verbs").

You really have to be there to appreciate Mr. Simmons' snappy, syncopated "All aboard." He pauses after the train's last destination and takes a breath before leaping on the first "a" in "all," holding it for a while, then lingering on the double l's. He then attacks the first "a" in "aboard," holds the "o" for the longest time and bites the word off at the end: "Haaallll haaboooo-wit!" It packs a wallop, and sometimes sets patrons of the adjacent Nedicks restaurant to running out with napkins flying.[6]

The writer manages to reproduce the sound of every letter in two words and convey them with an assist from great verbs (pauses, leaps, lingers, attacks, holds, bites, packs a wallop). This is the kind of detail to strive for.

When you are ready to sit down and write, you then have to decide which description to include, where to put it, and what to leave out. Here are a few observations and suggestions.

Be Highly Selective

Most beginning writers use too much description, thrown about too haphazardly. In the following example, it takes only three sentences to graphically convey several hours of rioting in San Francisco.

> What they attacked, finally, was City Hall. Gay leaders tried to lock arms, in a futile effort to protect the elaborate, domed building Harvey Milk so loved, but the smashing of the great glass doors set the full frenzy loose in the darkness, rocks and chunks of concrete flying, trash cans afire, branches ripped from trees, chants rising and breaking above the bullhorn appeals to calm. Police cars went up in flames, one by one, until burning squad cars lit the entire length of City Hall Plaza.[7]

Whether the action is violent as above, or benign, several hours can be reduced to several sentences through careful selection of detail. Here, a "typical" day for nannies in New York's Riverside Park is also handled in three well-chosen sentences.

> The nannies gather at the playground every day to talk of Pampers, prams and Presidential politics while watching the toddlers in their charge ride a myriad of plastic vehicles, swing on the swing set, and "socially interact": drooling on other children, poking fingers in their eyes, pulling hair, throwing a little sand in their faces, falling asleep in their presence and just generally having a fine time. Few of the nannies wear the old

starched white uniforms. They are too impractical, taking on the look of a painter's palette after 10 minutes with a toddler.[8]

In each of these disparate instances, the writers pack the activity of several hours into a brief paragraph. To do this, both focus on action: the rioters smashing great glass doors, throwing chunks of concrete, burning trash cans, desecrating trees; and in a more pastoral setting, children riding plastic vehicles, drooling, throwing sand. Both rely on long sentences laden with subordinate clauses to convey most of the information. And both, after panning the scene, use the last sentence to focus on one specific image that the writers feel most graphically represents the whole: police cars in flame; the nannies' dressing habits.

Zoom In on an Individual

This is especially helpful if you begin with a panoramic description, as above. Here is how another writer handled the description of five hundred Iowans who took a train ride to a benefit rock concert in Champaign, Illinois.

First, on the train:

> The train provided a leisurely, upbeat setting for the Iowans to get acquainted with one another. Hog farmers who wanted low grain prices chatted up grain farmers who wanted just the opposite. Country bankers went face to face with farmers on the edge of foreclosure. There were grain elevator operators, feed suppliers, combine salesmen, even an older woman from Churden who said her sales of Electrolux vacuum cleaners were way down.

Then, at the concert in the rain:

> As Tanya Tucker finished her set and X roared into theirs, the Iowans looked increasingly soggy and crestfallen, as they realized there would be a full 14 more hours of this stuff and that

no one was permitted to get back in after leaving the stadium. One man put bits of a balled-up napkin in his ears, stuck a toothpick in his mouth, and folded his arms over his belly, his eyes glazing over.[9]

To offset the broad strokes of this portrait, the writer gives us quick close-ups of Iowans picked from the crowd— the woman who sells vacuum cleaners, the bored man with paper in his ears. These snapshots lend variety and immediacy to the scene.

In the following feature about a soup kitchen, a writer showcases five people out of five hundred who came to have lunch one day in March.

Panorama:	Some of them simply file in and file out, picking up a bowl of soup and a bagel, eating it quickly, going their way.
Close-up #1:	But there is also *the Russian immigrant* in topcoat and fedora, a plaid scarf tucked beneath his long black beard, who eats and then sleeps sitting up in his chair.
Close-up #2:	There is *the young woman* with the backpack, dirty feet and dull eyes, who keeps going back for more bread,
Close-up #3:	and *the neatly dressed older man* who comes every day at 10 A.M. to help set up and stays until the linoleum is washed down in late af-
Panorama:	ternoon. Many stop to greet Mrs. Green or Father Frew as though they were the owners of a nice little bistro.
Close-up #4:	"Fine meal," said *one man,* shaking the
Close-up #5:	priest's hand, while *another* kissed Mrs. Green on one cheek and said, "Now you take care of yourself, O.K.? I'll see you Monday."
New close-up of #4:	Then the *first man* stood back and sang in a mellow baritone for a minute, "to pay for the meal." When he was finished, everyone applauded. "See, I'm a drunk, but I'm a nice drunk," he said with a smile.[10]

Showcase a Specific Person

This person can then symbolize a larger group. For example, once a year, about three thousand West Germans converge on a makeshift Wild West town in the German countryside to act out their passion for the American cowboy-and-Indian legends. To illustrate this phenomenon, this writer begins his feature by showcasing one of the three thousand participants.

> Joerg Lubadel thinks he has died and gone to Texas. His heroes have always been cowboys, and now here he is, sitting in Hank's Coffee Shop and looking every inch a cowboy himself.
>
> His long, thin frame is wrapped in the kind of full-length black coat that Western laymen used to wear. A gray-felt cowboy hat with a feather tucked in the band is cocked on his head, and a red-and-white trail rider's scarf hangs loosely around his neck. A holster with a shiny Colt revolver dangles on his right hip. On his feet, of course, are mud-caked boots. He swallows the last bite of grub and, before washing it down with a whiskey at the Golden Nugget Saloon across the street, digs out a Marlboro and a box of wooden matches from the pocket of his flannel shirt.
>
> "Watch this," he says. He strikes a match on the top of the wooden table once, twice, five more times. It doesn't light. Instead it snaps in two. One more strike and it snaps again.
>
> "Damn. I've seen them do it in the movies," he cusses. After making sure no one is watching, he produces a metal cigarette lighter, which works on the first flick. "I've got another one of these in my pocket, just in case," he whispers.[11]

Mr. Lubadel then disappears forever from the story. But he has served his purpose from the writer's perspective: he has given a human face to his feature.

When highlighting only a few people to represent many, however, it is very important to be fair, to select a person or variety of people who show the entire range of characters and not just a few who might support your particular prejudices.

When Describing Feelings, Show, Don't Tell

Or, as Mark Twain put it, "Don't say the old lady screamed. Bring her on the stage and make her scream." At the University of Wisconsin, Professor Emeritus Wilmott Ragsdale used to give journalism students the following advice about the reporting of emotions (those who heeded it went on to become some of the country's top journalists):

> When a character is said to be afraid, jealous, sexually excited, embarrassed, or hating, the reader or viewer will share the emotion only when enough of the particular *signs* of the emotion are given.
>
> The particular signs, the concrete instances, the facts given us are usually those that we get by way of our senses: things we see, hear, touch, taste, smell. We are given these specifics (symbols) in a sequence. Both the specifics themselves and the order in which we are given them will help determine the feelings that are aroused in us as we read or see.
>
> Hemingway seems to be speaking of this process when he says that he always sought "the real thing, the sequence of motion and fact which made the emotion."
>
> T. S. Eliot seems also to be speaking of this process in his essay on Hamlet: ". . . the only way of expressing emotion in art is by finding an 'objective correlative'; in other words, a set of objects; a situation, a chain of events which shall be the formula of that particular; such that when the general facts, which must terminate in sensory experience, are given, the emotion is immediately evoked."
>
> Ralph Waldo Emerson in his essay on "nature" also appears to be describing this same process: ". . . Every natural fact is a symbol of some spiritual fact. Every appearance in nature corresponds to some state of the mind, and that state of the mind can only be described by presenting that natural appearance as its picture." (nature)
>
> Nearly *every sort of writer chooses specifics and puts them in an order that will cause feelings in the reader.* There are both diffuse, sloppy feelings and precise, concentrated, accurate feelings.

> The skill with which the writer chooses the specifics and orders them determines how well he or she can communicate the feeling to the reader.[12]

Don't announce to the reader that the person you are describing is feeling a particular emotion (he felt sad; she felt nostalgic; they were furious), *unless you back it up with a specific example to show this feeling.*

For example, in describing customers in a chic New York drugstore, one beginning writer wrote: "All the women in the store were bored East Side matrons."

The problem here is that the writer has intruded into the story by telling the reader how *she* believes these shoppers feel. The writer has also committed the crime of overgeneralization. How does she know every woman in the store is not only bored, but also lives on the East Side of Manhattan and is married?

You can safely use a word like "bored" only if you support that contention with evidence—with specific illustrations of boredom. These may include yawns, tapping fingers, glazed eyes, nail-biting, chain-smoking.

And remember that even these acts may not necessarily reflect boredom. A person under stress may bite his nails; a shy person in a public place may seem listless and disinterested in people around her. When you interpret these acts as boredom, you risk losing credibility with the reader. It is better to just describe a few people doing things that reflect the mood of a situation, and let the reader reach into his or her own experiences for interpretation. This approach keeps the writer in the background. It lets the reader respond to the story, rather than to the writer's analysis of the story.

When it comes to emotions, it is unlikely that every person in a given situation is responding or acting in precisely the same way. If you write "all," it probably reflects a critical lack of attention to "each."

Be suspicious of yourself when you perceive an entire group of people as bored, happy, anxious, upset, excited. You may be the one who is feeling that way, or who would feel that way if you were in their situation. The same principle of caution applies when describing an individual. A woman who wipes her brow may be nervous, or just hot. A man who is laughing may be happy, or simply obsequious.

In the following description of visitors to the Vietnam Memorial in Washington, D.C., the writer does not say what the people at the memorial were feeling, only what they were doing. But the choice of description, if it is apt, will *evoke* some feelings in you, the reader.

> On Sunday, a World War II veteran came to attention and saluted; a farmer paused in front of a name, removed his John Deere cap and stood there fighting back tears; a mother placed a Polaroid shot of her two small children near the name of her husband and, drawing the children around her, quietly wept. Others, as they do almost every day, left behind a single rose, a wreath, a cross, a small American flag.[13]

These simple actions are universally understood to reflect the emotions of respect and grief. The use of these shared cultural signs helps arouse similar emotions in the reader.

Or consider this description of a photograph of a young man about to face tragedy.

> In only one of the pictures is Bernie alone. He is standing in a sunlit field of tall grass and flowers. He has on jeans and no shirt. His body is casually proud and muscular. He looks wistful and mellow, as if he knows a secret that would take too much effort to share. It's the kind of picture a girlfriend would have enlarged to put on her bulletin board.
>
> Bernie asked his sister Becky to take the photograph. She used the last frame on the roll. It is the last shot made of Bernie when he could stand alone.[14]

Soon after the picture was taken, swimming champion Bernie Jorn of Baltimore, Maryland, broke his neck in a diving accident at the age of seventeen and became a quadriplegic. The reporter who described Bernie's life before and after the accident chose this photograph as an effective vehicle to personalize the tragedy.

Wrap Description Around Strong Verbs

Reread chapter 3, "Verbs." Remember that description alone, with no redeeming action, stops the story in its tracks. If you use description with weak or passive verbs, be sure you are doing it *with intent* to create a special effect.

As in this lead, for example:

> It *is* noon in January in the high Arctic. The sun *went* down two months ago and *hasn't been seen* since. It *is* dark and foggy. The wind *blows* at 30 knots off the Arctic Ocean. The wind-chill factor *is* 50 degrees below zero.[15]

This lead itself is "cool," like the land it describes. The stagnant verbs, the stilted sentences, convey a sense of frozen isolation, unchanging terrain. They help to anchor the reader in this dark and lonely place, before moving into the feature.

But as a general rule, it is always better to weave description with action. You may not want to do this in every sentence, but it is a good idea to be generous with "action" sentences. This is especially difficult to do when describing what people are wearing. Notice how in this feature on a family reunion, the writer mixes descriptions of clothing with a few specific actions to keep it moving along.

> One of Aunt Rosalene's grandsons, sporting a straw cowboy hat that Willie Nelson himself would envy, *saunters* in with a good-looking girl in shorts. Three sisters from south Florida *wear* matching T-shirts that chronicle the event: "Clements Family Reunion '80." A long-haired college girl that someone says is a Sigma Nu sweetheart *strums* a guitar. Kids in cut-off

jeans and football jerseys *scamper* off through the pines to a nearby playground and swimming pool.[16]

These are quiet, almost gentle, sentences. The verbs are unobtrusive. But they make the difference: without their subtle help, the sentences would be lifeless on the page.

❑ DESCRIPTION EXERCISES

1. What's wrong with the following description? How can it be improved? Rewrite it.

> The brightly lit, cigarette-smoke–filled, two-room apartment, where wagers of $5 to $10,000 are made, is the site of a three-man bookmaking office, located in the Bay Ridge section of Brooklyn. Gamblers' bets come in to the office that operates seven days a week from noon to 2:00 P.M., and 6:00 P.M. to 8:00 P.M. on weekdays, and noon to 4:00 P.M. on weekends, over two black phones sitting on the large, wooden, scratched table in the uncarpeted, white-painted living room. Two men in their forties, Tony, short and muscular, and Vinny, tall and lanky, sit on black wooden folding chairs at the table, where streams of cigarette smoke rise from butt-filled ashtrays.

2. How can the description that follows be improved? Rewrite, condensing to one sentence.

> Thirty toned and fleshy bodies clad in thirty combinations of exercise attire scatter across the thick maroon and gold mat like litter on a windy day. They line the walls, pumping pulley weights or straining for the seventh sit-up.
>
> Some stand to bend, some sit to stretch, some lie on their sides and lift their legs to one-and-two-and routine or warm up, work out, cool down. Others mill about and schmooze. The air hangs, thick with dust and sweat. Fluorescent glare absorbs the dusk pouring in through huge caged windows and bathes the

tan brick walls of the gym in yellow haze. Clanking weights and squeaking overhead rings pierce the unusually heavy silence.

3. Go to a public place and write down careful descriptions of everything you see, hear, sense, and smell. Be a passive observer. Do not interview. Do not participate. Be sure to choose a place where you can spend an hour or two (but avoid libraries or other quiet places). Then write a 500-word story about the place, capturing its ambiance through appropriate (not excessive) detail. What major problems do you encounter in your writing? What details did you miss? Be sure to use good verbs to keep it moving.

Some examples of places you might go:

- a shopping mall
- a cafeteria
- an airport, bus, or train departure lounge
- an exercise salon
- a garage sale
- the information booth of a large store
- a children's playground
- a parade
- a town hall or city council meeting

□ **5** □

QUOTES

QUOTES ARE POWERFUL ALLIES. A good quote should reverberate. It should have resonance. It should set your story on edge. A good quote should reveal the quoted person's beliefs, motives, secrets, whims, hidden agendas, pain, sense of humor, philosophy, erudition, expertise, passion, ignorance, or fatal flaw. It you dislike a person, you can dangle her from the noose of her own words. If you admire someone, you can endear him to the reader through a few well-turned quotes.

But, like description, a little bit goes a long way. Let quotes do the work *only* when you cannot find a better stylistic tool to do it for you.

Use quotes sparingly. Few people are highly quotable, and the best-written profiles contain only a light sprinkling of quotes. Don't lean on quotes. Never put in a quote something you can paraphrase better in your own words, such as statistics or basic background information like:

"My grandfather was a miller in Sherburne, N.Y., and he always had a few trotting horses. He owned them, bred them, and raced them in the county fair circuits."

The factual, the obvious, the oblique, and the just plain boring should be condensed and paraphrased by the writer. Remember that quotes are another form of color. Use them with wisdom and discretion to maximize effectiveness.

The Best Kinds of Quotes

Here are a few ways in which quotes can best be used:

1. To Praise.   Here, a physician comments on a colleague's career:

"Rod even way back was the ultimate physician," [he] says. ... "It's just a gift, like a football player who runs fast. He has that gift, a gift of caring and true compassion, all the good qualities, and we all recognized it."[1]

2. To Convey Loss.   This widow is almost inarticulate in her mourning, yet the pain of her loss comes through:

"If he was forgotten, I think I would have felt worse," she said, as some of the police officers stooped to kiss her cheek. "I miss him—forget it, I can't explain it to you. You try to get on with your life and—forget it, I can't talk about what it's like."[2]

When a 29-year-old man from Slade, Kentucky, pleaded guilty to second-degree murder in the torture and killing of a couple in their home, a reporter gathered comments from the man's relatives, friends, and former teachers. The sense of a beloved child gone astray heightens the horror of the story.

The father:

"I know my son didn't kill these people. All I want to do is help my son."

The mother in tears in her kitchen:

"Oh, my God . . . Oh, my God. They did this to that poor woman."

The teacher:

"Oh, sure, I remember Charlie. I dearly loved that child . . . If you see Charlie, tell him I still love him," she said. "It's too bad."[3]

Any sense of loss—whether fleeting or permanent—is usually best conveyed by the person who has gone through the experience. Take, for instance, the rather mundane experience of parents saying good-bye to a child leaving for summer camp. This reporter captured the ambivalence that tugs at many parents' hearts:

Mr. Mandel, who talks much about the carefree, childless life, recalled clutching his 9-year-old son at the bus and his son finally saying: "Dad, can I please get on the bus now?"

"Half of you," said Mr. Mandel, "wants him to be confident and independent and the other half of you wants him to say 'I can't go, I love you too much.' I just have the feeling all the time like something is missing." . . .

"He's been gone two weeks and a little more than a day now."[4]

3. *To Express Reaction to Trauma.* Martha Howard Bremner, a 22-year-old burn victim from Rockford, Ill., who spent nine weeks in the hospital undergoing excruciating

therapy and surgery, tells what she has learned from her ordeal:

> "I know there's a God and there's a purpose for my being here. And I know I won't go to hell—because I've already been there."[5]

4. To Convey Private Opinion About a Public Situation.
This is a good way to air reactions that reporters cannot, or should not, express on their own.

When Delta Air Lines pilots committed four major, potentially fatal mistakes in two weeks, this writer used a telephone call to Delta from a customer—an elderly Mississippi woman—to make a point:

> In a frail but polite voice, [she] explained how she had flown no other airline but Delta for the last 33 years.
> Then she paused, dropped her voice and said: "Now you tell me, sir, what in the hell is going on over there?"[6]

An FBI agent had this to say about organized crime in Las Vegas:

> "When I'm told there is no organized crime representative in Las Vegas, that's ridiculous on its face. I laugh at 'em. You have to accept those kinds of statements for what they're worth, and they're worth nothing."[7]

An irate Russian, upon finding out that the new American pizza truck parked on the banks of Moscow River did not accept rubles, gave this comment to a reporter:

> "We hear all about these great Western things they are bringing here," said Mr. Bogdanov, sulking after his unsuccessful attempt to sample what was billed as the first American pizza in the Soviet Union. "But then it turns out that you have to

buy these things with Western currency, meaning you have to be a Westerner to buy it. Great. Now we can actually see things that we still can't have."⁸

5. To Let People Describe Their Own Work, Hobby, or Life-style, Provided They Do it in a Pithy Way. Here's how one man describes the bar he owns on the banks of the Rosebud River in Jimtown, Montana:

"I'm the fifth owner of this joint. The first was a guy named Jim Ellison. That's how the place came to be Jimtown. It isn't a town. I guess you noticed this is the only thing here, this saloon. Isn't it the worst place you ever saw?"⁹

Or who but an experienced farmer can better describe the sinister seductions of heavy farm machinery?

"Machinery can be intoxicating. You sit there on top of a huge tractor, rolling across those fields, and you feel like God. It's an amazing feeling, and a real one, and I think some people get so they don't feel complete without it.

"That's one of the reasons they keep buying bigger and bigger tractors, these enormous four-wheel drives, tearing up and down the fields. Tearing up and down. They are incredibly expensive machines; they'll run you $16 an hour in fuel alone, and you can do in one day what used to take you three or four—but then the question arises, are you doing anything useful on the three or four you saved? You buy this gigantic machine with its incredible capability and all of a sudden, you're done.

"And you start thinking, 'My God, if I bought another 600 acres I could do that, too.' So you buy it, and then you find if you only had a bigger machine, you could buy even more. At the end of it, you're doing 2,000 acres on this fantastic Star Wars machinery and you're so far in debt that if anything goes wrong—and I mean if they stop eating soy sauce in Ireland—you lose the whole works, including the place you started with."¹⁰

During the Feast of St. Francis of Assisi, a reporter interviewed the proud owner of a show elephant named Mignon outside the Cathedral of St. John the Divine in New York shortly before the pachyderm walked down the aisle for her annual blessing.

> "Mignon's feeling good today," said Bob Comerford, whose livestock travels the county and state fair circuit. "She's just acting up to shock people. Minnie's a pro. Yesterday she was in Newport at a church fair giving rides, and tomorrow she goes to Vermont for a hardware store promotion. This elephant has done it all. She's done opera—the triumphal march in *Aïda,* she did in Hartford, Cleveland and Salt Lake City. She's been in *Vogue.* She's filmed dozens of commercials. The one where an elephant steps on a Tonka truck? That's Minnie. I can't even remember everything Minnie has stepped on."[11]

6. To Highlight a Person's Philosophy, from the Insightful to the Insipid. A female chief justice of the California Supreme Court had this to say about being "first":

> "I've always said that when you're the first of your sex or your race in a position, three things apply to you," she says. "One— you're placed under a microscope. Two—you're allowed no margin for error. And three—the assumption is always made that you achieved your position on something other than merit."[12]

When Sidney Biddle Barrows, member of a prestigious family that traces its lineage to the *Mayflower,* was arrested and charged with running a high-class prostitution service in New York City, a relative expounded on Ms. Barrows's philosophy, passed down from her father.

> "Sidney," her father had told her. "Whatever you do, pay your income tax, that's how they got Al Capone. There are a whole bunch of people in prison who committed murders, and the

only reason they're there is because they didn't pay their income tax.

"No matter what you do in this world, pay your income tax and get yourself a good accountant."[13]

"Philosophy" need not be profound or even very pragmatic. A maven of neighborhood yard sales had this to say about her weekend experiences:

"My philosophy is, when in doubt, buy," said Loretta. "I've often been sorry about what I didn't get, but I've never regretted what I did."

A shopping companion added his own yard-sale folk wisdom:

"I'll let you in on another rule. You can sell almost anything at a garage sale, but there's three things you can't even GIVE away: Reader's Digest Condensed Books, aluminum Christmas trees, and cracked bowling balls. Everyone hates carting them around as much as you do."[14]

7. To Say Anything Outrageous or Provocative. It adds extra punch, for example, to let an Orthodox rabbi carry on this way about the high cost of kosher food:

"Kosher doesn't taste any better; kosher isn't healthier; kosher doesn't have less salmonella," Rubin said. "Religion is not based on logic. You can eat a Holly Farm chicken and not know the difference. But a Holly Farm chicken sells for 39 cents a pound on sale. Kosher chicken, especially right before the holidays, can sell for $1.69 a pound."[15]

It packs an extra wallop when an incumbent Republican President weighs the value of bread over bullets:

Every gun that is made, every warship launched, every rocket fired, signifies in the final sense a theft from those who hunger and are not fed, those who are cold and are not clothed."[16]

8. To Show Interaction Between People. Dialogue is the stuff of high and low drama, in life as in art. Used carefully, it can lend a theatrical touch to a feature. Here, a writer uses teacher-student dialogue from a class in which stockbrokers are taught to get new clients over the phone:

> "Ring, ring," says a broker, pretending he is making a "cold call" to a hot prospect, played by Mr. Good.
> "Hello," Mr. Good says, in a tone that would freeze boiling oil.
> "Is Mr. Good there?" the broker asks tentatively.
> "No, he's not, you simpering wimp!" The class breaks into laughter.
> "Is Mr. Good there?" doesn't sound authoritative, Mr. Good explains. "May I speak with Mr. Good, please" is better, he says, making it sound like a command instead of a request. The trick is to raise the pitch of your voice as you said "Good." Then drop it like a bowling ball as you say "please."[17]

Dialogue can also show a *failure* to communicate. Here, a husband and wife fight over their Christmas tree:

> "You want a fake tree," a woman looking at trees at Broadway and 91st Street was saying to her spouse, "you get a fake tree. It's your decision."
> "I don't want a fake tree," the spouse said, "but the artificial trees just seem to make a lot more sense."
> "Then get a fake one," the woman said, and muttered something about serving Spam for Christmas dinner.[18]

9. To Reveal Personality. Motivations, attitudes, personal concerns and commitments, emotional problems, an indomitable sense of humor—all ooze through the surface of a good quote.

For example, here is a quote from a Wisconsin man who bought 35 woodland acres and then learned that hundreds of containers of toxic wastes had been buried under the access road running through his property. When state officials told him they not only expected him to pay for removing the waste, but also expected him to sue the people who had dumped it there originally, the reporter lets him describe his sense of helplessness.

> "All I wanted was a nice quiet place that had a lot of deer and racoons and things on it so I could take my family there on outings. I'm afraid of what may be out there under that road and how I'm going to pay for cleaning it up. I've never been involved in anything like this before."[19]

Or, in a feature on residents of a state mental hospital, the reporter focuses on one inmate, 20-year-old "Mary," who, the reporter says, "jumps subjects quickly and randomly." To support this contention, the reporter illustrates with a quote:

> "Uhh-mmmm," she makes a sound in her throat, and grins an impish grin. "Excuse me. I was just wondering, are you writing a book?
>
> "I've been writing since I was 10 years old. I want to be a songwriter or a singer or a disc jockey on a radio station or a fashion model or an actress.
>
> "What's your sign?"
>
> Her fingernails are painted red. Manicures are tricky when your hands shake from medication. In places she has as much polish on her skin as on her nails.
>
> "My parents are separated," she says. "My father's an alcoholic. He has his own problems so he doesn't have too much time for me, but I still love him. I sent him a drawing today."[20]

When it comes to humor, consider the words of author Mickey Spillane, who had cryptic words for a critic who lambasted the reading public for putting seven of Spillane's books on the top ten paperback best-seller list at the same time: "Shut up," Spillane warned, "or I'll write three more." Spillane added that critics don't hurt him as long as they "don't rip up my dollar bills." He then wondered:

> "Why did all these giants [critics] descend on me and my little stories? I wasn't doing anything of national import. All I was trying to do was entertain the public and make a buck. If there was no money in writing, I wouldn't write. I'm a commercial writer, not an 'author.' Margaret Mitchell was an author. She wrote one book."[21]

10. To Highlight the Drama of a Past Event.   Someone who was on the scene as witness, victim, or participant can often, in his or her own words, convey the moment in a more forceful and immediate way.

The plane crash survivor recalls the first time she flew again. When she entered the plane,

> "that's when I really started having problems. My heart really started pounding as fast as it could with the Valiums [a tranquilizer] in my system. I got teary and embarrassed and then, before everybody got on the plane, the pilot came back and introduced himself and said we had clear skies ahead for the landing.
>
> "I just shut my eyes and said to Dad, 'Don't tell me anything.' I guess I cried. I cried while we were landing because I was so darned scared, because I knew we were getting closer and closer to the ground. But I didn't want to look. You don't have any idea what goes on with my stomach and my brain on landing. You know, it'll probably always be that way.
>
> "Anyhow, all of a sudden we touched down and I cried and hugged Dad again. The people across from me looked at me and said, 'Good job.' They were just proud of me, but not half as proud as my Dad."[22]

11. To Back Up Unsubstantiated Statements.   For the most part, statistics should be used only in paraphrase. But there are exceptions.

An article on the problems facing the juvenile justice system makes the point that children who commit crimes often become criminals as adults.

The writer is careful to let an "expert," such as a criminal court judge, support this view with a quote.

> "Fully 90 percent of the people I sentence as adults, people charged with rape or murder or some other horrible crime, have had problems as juvenile offenders," he said. "That is why I say the only way to significantly cut into adult crime is to cut into juvenile crime."[23]

All the above quotes share three common traits.

First, they *lend credence* to the story by providing inside information or opinion. Only a fond teacher could say of an indicted murderer: "If you see Charlie, tell him I still love him." Only an angry airline passenger could say to the company: "What in the hell is going on over there?"

Second, they make the story feel *immediate.* A good quote moves the reader into the heart of the story. The reporter is no longer the obvious gatekeeper between reader and event. Instead, the reader comes face to face with another person's experiences and beliefs.

And third, with the exception of quotes used to back up unsubstantiated statements, all quotes evoke some *emotion*—bemusement, empathy, sadness, annoyance, humor. That, at least, is the aim. Even the funniest quote is probably not going to tickle every funny bone; even the most poignant comment is not going to send a shiver up every spine. But they should strike home 90 percent of the time.

How To Handle Quotes in Copy

Sometimes a quote that seems good when you hear it falls flat when you read it. This can happen when the writer fails to provide enough *context*—the background information or ambiance pertinent to the quote.

You must be sure your quotes are anchored solidly in the story. Even the best of quotes will lay limp on the page unless they are "set up" properly. What precedes and follows the quote is often as important as the quote itself. Quotes must be highlighted properly or they will be lost on the page.

To set up a quote, the writer needs to prepare the reader in the previous sentence or paragraph. Take, for example, the feature on the Maryland man who became a quadriplegic at age 17. First, the writer sums up the small daily experiences that this young man will never again have. The writer, in effect, distills in a few phrases a lifetime of loss.

> He misses the little things most, things that would better define him as Bernie. A certain walk, a certain stance, a gesture, a firm handshake. To give someone the thumbs up sign, to clap at a concert, to reach over and put his arm around a girl.

Then the writer uses *one single quote,* to highlight this deprivation:

> "I'll never forget the first time I realized in the hospital I wouldn't be able to hug somebody. A physical therapist was gonna transfer me. I leaned up against her for the transfer and it felt so good to be close to somebody I started crying."[24]

Occasionally, it is more effective to use a quote *followed* by an anchor, as in this story about a mother who was caring at home for her 20-month-old baby, who had been in a coma for 5 months:

> "I'd rather have him die at home where he's surrounded by people who love him than get a 3 a.m. call from some hospital," Mrs. Vermilling says. She is adjusting a row of stuffed

animals propped up on the edge of Shawn's bed. One of them is Wish Bear, the Care Bear that helps children's wishes come true.[25]

Here, this single description following the quote highlights the poignancy of the situation.

This pattern—supporting a quote up front or in back with a paraphrase, a description, or a summation—is used all the time by experienced feature writers. As a "lay" reader, you shouldn't notice it. As a professional writer, you must use it.

This support system can (and should) be repeated through a story. Here is an example of how it works in a story about the National Weather Service offices in New York City.

The Setup:	Between the computers, the radar, the satellites and his own meteorologists, says Mr. Gibson, the Weather Service is usually correct, except for the occasional macroblunder.
The Quote:	"With all the new technology, we don't often make medium-sized errors," he said. "Either it's so small it's almost insignificant, or it's monumental."
The Setup:	The staff members in Mr. Gibson's office are still chagrined about the big snowstorm predicted for the city three weekends back, the one that fizzled into a translucent haze of slush on the sidewalks.
The Quote:	"We don't know exactly what went wrong," Mr. Gibson said. "See that big stack of weather maps? That's it. We've done a dozen postmortems on that one."
The Setup:	Mr. Gibson thinks it might have been a warm eddy of water in the ocean near New York Harbor that caused the snow to go elsewhere, but he won't swear to it.
The Quote:	"No excuses," he said.[26]

What to Do with Lots of Quotes

If you find yourself face to face with a notebook full of quotes from, say, a luncheon speech, a court proceeding, or a long interview, consider these possible ways of handling them before you just give up and repeat them verbatim in the story, risking an editor's scorn and your reader's boredom.

1. Use Partial Quotes. Often, you can integrate a few words of direct quotes into copy without breaking the flow. By placing these partial quotes carefully in the story, you can give added emphasis to a scene. Consider this partial quote, from a feature about a riot in San Quentin prison, during which three prison guards and two prisoners were shot or stabbed to death.

> [The warden] remembers with some precision how he told the guard's wife that her husband was dead, and how her daughters came home afterward, not yet knowing, and the wife knelt to give them crackers to eat. "As though she were giving them communion," the warden says.[27]

2. Sum Up in Your Own Words. During a luncheon to promote the city of Pittsburgh, the writer took dutiful notes and then carefully shaped his own condensed version of the event.

> One after another, members of the group said investors and media buyers should know that Pittsburgh was no longer the grimy, shot-and-a-beer place one might think, but was, rather, something of an earthly paradise, to hear them tell it, a heavenly place of more green trees and safer streets than any other large city, of a vibrant economy and a renowned symphony, of the finest schools and the best sports teams, and of the nicest, most "upscale" people one would ever want to meet.

Even the speech by the mayor is summed up in one line:

> The Mayor told of his campaign to strike back at wisecracks
> Howard Cosell was making about the city and said he would
> like to gather every textbook in the country and tear out the
> pictures of Pittsburgh, which he said invariably are of smoke-
> stacks.[28]

**3. String a Few Brief Quotes Together, for Star Bill-
ing.** Note how this writer uses three consecutive quotes effectively in her day-in-the-life profile of a traffic officer.

> In a city where parking illegally may someday classify as an
> outdoor sport, Officer Butcher's life is filled with the following
> lines:
> "I'll just be here for a minute."
> "The sign says you can't park here."
> "I'm a good 10 inches from the hydrant."[29]

4. Set the Quotes Apart with Graphics. In a prophetic profile
of Senator Gary Hart of Colorado, which was published long
before his extramarital dalliance ended his chance at the 1988
presidency, the writer interviewed Hart's friends and colleagues, and then highlights the most revealing of the quotes.
To do this, he omits them from the main body of the story and
puts them in italics in boxes surrounded by extra white space.
A sample:

> "Gary is very idealistic. I am a lot more realistic about what can
> be done. I still care, but I also care about my mortgage these
> days. It's part of growing up. He hasn't grown up yet in that
> regard."

> "He had a marvelous mix of ambition combined with a real
> sense of mission; there is a lot of priest, minister and rabbi in
> Gary Hart. He is intense. Sometimes I think he's too intense.
> I worry about him as a friend."[30]

Thoughts on Altering a Quote

The general rule is: never change a quote. Never take a quote out of context in a way that changes its meaning. The exception is: within limits, it is reasonable to clean up someone's grammar if it seems unfair to the person to retain embarrassing spoken grammatical errors.

Here is how an editor at the *Houston Chronicle* explains his policy on cleaning up quotes:

> Yes, we clean up grammar and syntax when it is obvious that the speaker has more than a nodding acquaintance with the English language. Also we avoid quoting dialect for the most part (we're gonna do this or that). . . . We don't have enough apostrophes to handle all the runnin' and funnin' and sunnin' that goes on in the Sunbelt.

Here is the *Philadelphia Inquirer*'s policy:

> Generally direct quotations are not altered in the editing process. However, we repair minor grammatical errors in direct quotations unless those errors are pertinent to the news—or are deemed to be extremely important in reporting color. We should fix such minor errors especially in cases when they might take on undue importance and cause the speaker to look foolish. However, we would not change a quotation simply because of an error in agreement with an antecedent, for example, since such errors are accepted in colloquial speech. Mispronunciations, such as "gonna" for "going to," are corrected, as they are acceptable to common speech but make a speaker appear to be inarticulate when rendered in writing.[31]

However, there are bona fide occasions when it behooves the writer to retain errors of grammar or syntax: to show regional differences in speech, to reflect a foreign accent, to show a lack of education. But to retain these differences in speech patterns demands careful note-taking. When some visitors from France gave their view of American sports and television, the reporter noticed their tendency to use the modifier "the" in front of English nouns as they would with French nouns. By keeping this speech pattern in the final draft, the reader can almost "hear" the French accent.

> Sometimes they watch television and try to understand it. "We watch the baseball," Mr. Gres said, "and they are with the clubs and the running. And there is the American football and they jump on top of each other and then get off, time after time."
>
> "And on the news programs there is no analysis," Mr. Fiers said, "just the murder, the fire, the accident; the murder, the fire, the accident."
>
> "And so much publicity!" said Mr. Fiers, speaking of advertising. "You are watching the dramatic production and the hero is chasing to help the beautiful woman and all of a sudden there is a man selling the hamburgers."[32]

A Colorado reporter who interviewed some recent immigrants from Indochina also chose to retain their grammatical errors. It seems appropriate; their struggles with the English language become a part of their many struggles to survive in a new culture.

Van Nguyen, the owner of a Vietnamese restaurant, says:

> "I made a big mistake. . . . First of all, I thought it easy, but it not easy. I think, if open business, I have American customer—I make money because American people, they like to go out often . . ."
>
> Nguyen feels guilty that her children must help her between their jobs and school work. "Sometimes I feel sorry I open this place. I think . . . I help them, but I don't. They have to help me. Sometimes I see them study 2 or 3 o'clock in morning and I feel sorry, but nothing I can do."[33]

When a 19-year-old drifter committed suicide in her jail cell in Norfolk, Virginia, a local reporter pieced together as much as she could of the young woman's life.

An unmailed letter, found in her cell, is quoted: "I don't really care if you or any of my family doesn't keep in touch," the letter said. "When I need y'all, y'all ain't there."

And a family member is also quoted: "She weren't given any help when she needed it. . . . There was just nothing nobody could do."[34]

Errors of grammar can add to our information about a person's history and life-style. In this last example, for instance, one could extrapolate that the teenager came from a rural Southern family with little formal education. One could be wrong; but grammar can be a clue to a person's past.

How To Get Good Quotes: Thirteen Steps to Success[35]

Be judged not by your answers but by your questions.
—ADAPTED FROM VOLTAIRE

1. Be in Good Mental Shape.   An interview demands alertness, quick responses, and good instincts. This means your mind and your equipment—whether it is a tape recorder or a pen and notepad—should be in good working order. If you are sluggish in an interview, you will get sluggish quotes. The interview is a formal ritual, like a waltz, and the interviewer must take the lead. Don't go to an interview tired, distracted, or ill-prepared.

2. Be Punctual.   Allow enough time for rush-hour traffic jams. It is better to arrive early, have a cup of coffee, review your notes, and focus on the interview, rather than to dash in at the last minute.

3. Be Self-Confident. When you arrive, *act confident,* even if you don't feel it. Beginning writers often feel the person being interviewed is doing them a big favor by "granting" the interview. It is true that you, the interviewer, are there to learn; the interviewee is there to reveal and explain. However, remember that this is a two-way street. Something is in it for both of you. People want their names in print, their positions explained, their contributions—great or small—to be understood and appreciated by family, friends, enemies, and posterity. It is understandable to be nervous during an interview—even the most experienced interviewer feels it. But that nervous energy is an ally; it will help keep you on your toes. Also remember that the person being interviewed probably feels nervous too.

4. Do Your Research. For national public figures, access to background information is easy. Go to the databases, or to the newspaper index or the magazine index in your library, and pull out the relevant clips. (See chapter 8, "Doing It" for more on research tools and techniques.) For local public figures, you might have to do a bit more digging, since it is unlikely that stories on them will have been indexed. In that case, a friendly local reporter or editor can help you find what you need.

Stories on issues require the same kind of advance research as stories on prominent individuals. Know what has already been printed. This will make your questions—and the answers to them—more specific.

Features on private persons—the heroic firefighter, the owner of the new clothing store, the farmer who just declared bankruptcy—may not be researchable. But you can get any needed background information in the course of the interview, which you can then check later with neighbors, friends, employers, or in the public records.

5. Have an Angle Going into the Interview. It is always better to approach an interview subject with a specific angle in mind. Instead of: "I would like to talk to you about your career," it is better to say: "I would like to talk about why your show went off the air even though the ratings were high." Instead of: "I would like to talk to you about your life," it is better to say: "I would like to hear how your life has changed now that (you're famous/you're a father, etc.)." Your angle may change during the course of the interview, and that's okay. But you need a handle going in; otherwise your interview is likely to slide all over the place, and so will your story. It is also far less intimidating for the person being interviewed to be told the interview is focused on a narrow aspect of his or her life. Most people find it overwhelming to think of recounting an entire life, or career, in a single interview. They may end up doing that, but don't tell them you expect it.

6. Ask Good Questions. This means knowing how to ask questions in a way to get good answers.

Don't ask yes-no questions, because they produce yes-no answers. For example:

> AVOID: So is it true you plan to run for state senator in the next election?

> ASK: What is involved in your decision about whether to run for state senator in the next election?

The first question begs for a yes-no answer, and then you will need to ask a series of follow-up questions to try and move the person toward a more thoughtful and compelling quote. The second question forces the person to give a more articulate and reflective answer.

> AVOID: Do you feel happy about being told you just won the Nobel Prize (or the lottery, or a trip to Hawaii)?

ASK: *How do you feel* about being told you just won the Nobel Prize?

Again, the first question will produce a yes-no answer. And, just as bad, it projects the writer's reaction to a situation onto the interviewee. The writer assumes winning is conducive to happy feelings. In fact, the subject could be feeling a range of other emotions: fear, scorn, anxiety and ambivalence, as well as joy.

7. Don't be Afraid to Say "I don't understand," or "Could you give me an example?" People are often oblique and unclear when they talk, which produces oblique and unclear quotes. It is all right to stop someone in the middle of an interview and ask for clarification or an explanation. Blame it, if you must, on your own inability to understand the obvious. At worst, this will make the interviewee feel superior to you, and may even lead to some condescending remark; this is most often done by people who feel insecure about what they are saying in the first place, so don't take it to heart. It happens to the best of writers.

The point is to get a good quote, not to earn the undying esteem of the person you're interviewing. At best, asking for an example or a simpler explanation will force the interviewee to clarify thoughts that may still be vague in her or his own mind; it will give you better quotes, and you will be able to write a better story.

8. Ask Follow-up Questions. Go into the interview with half a dozen questions typed or written out *clearly* and keep that list in front of you. Leave space between questions on the list, so that as the interviewee is answering one question, you can jot down the new questions being triggered by the answers. That way, if you can't get to the follow-up question right away, you can go back to it before the end of the interview. If you don't write it down, you may forget it.

9. Go from the General to the Specific. It is always best to start with pleasantries at the beginning of an interview and save the Killer Questions for near the end. Talk about the weather, the interviewee's family pictures on the desk, the view—anything to break the ice and help the interviewee (and yourself) feel comfortable and get some sense of one another before you proceed. Begin gently.

Investigative writer Jessica Mitford suggests you list your questions in graduated form from Kind to Cruel. "Kind questions," she explains, "are designed to lull your quarry into a conversational mood."[36]

As you proceed, you can become more specific and aggressive in your questions, if it is called for. For effective interview tactics, read some interviews by Oriana Fallaci, Jessica Mitford, and John McPhee (see "Appendix: Read Well to Write Well," page 207). Your own tactics will depend in large part on your own personality—what style you feel comfortable with—and the personality of your subject. As a general rule, it is better not to force a false interview style on yourself: if you are the quiet, persistent type, don't force yourself to bully people into answers; if you are the bullying type, don't pretend to be sweet and patient. You should modify your approach to suit your subject, but if you are not being honest in your own interview style, chances are the interviewee will pick that up and be less than honest in his or her answers. Be professional. Be, like a good Scout, prepared. You have a better chance of getting what you need.

10. Don't Shy away from Embarrassing Questions. Ask the questions your mother told you never to ask ("How much money do you make?" "Why did you leave your husband?" "How do you feel about sex now that you're 80?"). Save it for near the end, however. The worst that can happen is that the interviewee will refuse to answer, or will kick you out. Usually, however, he or she will answer.

11. Be a Good Listener. One of the main interviewing faults of beginning writers is that they talk too much. You don't have to impress the interviewees with how smart you are—your questions will do that. If your subject hesitates, or pauses, don't always butt in with a comment, or a new question. Let a little silence fill the room. Most people are uncomfortable with silence in this kind of situation, and will fill it up by talking. Under this kind of pressure, interview subjects have been known to blurt out the most interesting and incriminating comments. Interrupt only to get back on track, or for amplification. To check on your own listening capacities, tape an interview and then play it back, listening for the number of times you interrupted. If it is more than three to four times in a half-hour interview, you may not be giving your interviewees enough slack.

12. Take Prodigious Notes. This applies even if you are using a tape recorder. Be sure to take notes of physical details: how the subject lit her cigarette; the way he leaned back in his chair; whether she drinks her coffee black. These details, when correlated with what the person is saying at the time, are essential for adding color to the feature story. Otherwise, you're left with a string of quotes, and no description upon which to hang them. (See "How To Handle Quotes in Copy," page 89.)

Even if you prefer to use a tape recorder, cover yourself by taking notes of the key comments made in the interview. This way, you have some backup in case your recorder breaks down (and every experienced interviewer has at least one such horror story). Also, relying on a tape recorder tends to deaden your perceptions in an interview: it is like turning on the television set and waiting to be entertained. Taking notes helps keep you alert, engaged in the give-and-take of the interview.

Beginning interviewers are often embarrassed about looking down to take notes: it defies the usual social nicety of

looking someone in the eye and nodding attentively as the
person bares his or her soul. While it may seem awkward to
you, it does not seem offensive to the person being interviewed. On the contrary, it is rather disconcerting to see someone taking notes without looking down (how *will* they read
that scribble later on?) and more alarming to be interviewed
and see the person *not* taking notes (is none of what I'm saying
worth anything?). So, scribble away. And don't be afraid to
ask the person to slow down so you can catch up, or to repeat
a particularly compelling comment. While many reporters do
not know shorthand, most develop their own shortcuts in
note-taking. Develop some for yourself.

A word about tape recorders: tape recorders are wonderful. How did we ever do without them? However, many
people who are not used to being interviewed will freeze
when they see a tape recorder. Be sure to ask if they mind
being taped. Some people, not wanting to offend, will say they
don't mind, and will freeze anyway. If you suspect that is
happening, turn off the tape recorder during the interview.

Tape recorders are particularly useful if you want a legal
record. Although written notes are valid in court, nothing
beats having the person's own words available for replay.
They are also useful when the person being interviewed is a
fast talker, is particularly articulate, or is using terminology
with which you are not familiar. The down side, however, is
that someone—probably you—will have to transcribe the
tape, which can take two to three times as long as the interview
itself. If you are on assignment for a magazine, you might ask
that the cost of a transcriber be included in your expenses.
Newspapers, however, will as a general rule not pay for this
service.

13. End Well. Your last question should be: "Do you have
anything to add?" Often, you have overlooked something that
is pertinent. Sometimes, the subject is eager to unburden

something that you would have no way of knowing about—
unless you give him or her carte blanche to talk about it.

Your last statement should be: "I may be calling you with
a few follow-up questions, once I've reviewed my notes." This
clears the way for future contact: you don't have to feel embarrassed about calling back; and the subject, having been forewarned, won't be surprised to hear from you again.

❏ QUOTE EXERCISES

1. Clip from your local or state newspaper, or from a magazine, a feature that contains six or more quotes. Check them
against the guidelines in this chapter for effective usage:

> **A.** What purpose does each quote serve? Each quote should
> do at least one of the following, or it probably does not
> belong in the story.
>
> - praises
> - conveys loss
> - expresses reaction to trauma
> - conveys private opinion about a public situation
> - lets people describe their own work, hobby, or life-style
>   in a pithy way
> - highlights a person's philosophy
> - expresses something outrageous or provocative
> - shows interaction between people
> - reveals personality
> - highlights the drama of a past event
> - backs up an unsubstantiated statement
>
> **B.** In what way does each quote lend credence to the story?
> **C.** In what way does each quote make the story feel more
> immediate?
> **D.** What emotion is evoked by each quote?

2. Using the quotes from the first exercise, look at how they are handled in the feature. Each quote should be aided by one or more of the following techniques:

- It is "set up" in advance with a paraphrase, a description, a summation.
- It is anchored after the quote with a paraphrase, a description, or a summation.
- It is a partial quote.
- It is summed up in the writer's own words.
- Brief quotes are strung together for star billing.
- The quotes are set apart graphically for emphasis.

A. Are the quotes grammatically correct? If not, should they be corrected? Why or why not?

B. Did the writer ask good, specific questions to get these quotes? Why or why not? Use one quote to illustrate your answer.

C. How would you improve the quotes in the article you have chosen?

D. What additional quotes would you suggest the writer get?

E. What quotes would you take out?

3. Interview a person about his or her job, or hobbies, or some other specific personal subject. Here are examples of people interviewed by students in a feature writing class, which you can adapt for your local community:

- the owner of a tattoo parlor
- a music therapist
- the owner of a mozzarella cheese factory
- a person who sells cold-weather gear for dogs
- the organizer of the annual Halloween parade
- a diamond cutter
- a funeral home director
- the publisher of the local community paper

- the disc jockey of a popular radio station
- a bank guard
- the manager of a college dormitory

Now write a profile based on the interview. Keep it short—fewer than 1,000 words. Be careful not to overquote in the profile.

A. What problems do you encounter in trying to write up this profile? Do you have too many quotes? Are they specific enough? What follow-up questions should you ask to beef up your story?

B. Do a follow-up interview based on the problems you encountered your first time around, and rewrite.

VOICE

EVEN THE SIMPLEST FEATURE has several layers. Beneath the factual "denoted message" of the story lies a series of "connoted messages" based on your prejudices, sympathies, education, sense of humor, erudition, and limitations. These connoted messages are implicit in the story.

They constitute your *voice*—active, aggressive, woven into the very fabric of your nonfiction.

In previous chapters, you have seen how the lead, the verb, the description, or the quote can convey a subliminal message that is intended to evoke responses, conscious or subconscious, to your story.

But a single stylistic technique alone does not always give you voice. Your overall success at finding the voice for your story depends ultimately on the way you blend all the ingredients of your story. It depends on your ability to massage language to suit your needs. Take this story about a homeless 65-year-old woman:

"I have suffered, oh, no one knows what I have suffered,"
moaned Sally, holding her head with a gesture that would have
brought Sarah Bernhardt to her knees.

Sally says she has been beaten, robbed, mugged and
stabbed. She also once swallowed a cockroach, an experience
of unrelieved horror, except that a priest had enough presence
of mind to give her a long slug of wine to wipe out the taste.
Sally is not an alcoholic, but she confides with an air of can-
dor that would do Mary Pickford proud, "I do like apricot
brandy . . ."

According to Sally, What She Has Suffered all started when
her father's brother told him there was gold in the streets of
America. "Like a fool, he believed it," she said.[1]

The author has found several ways to reveal her own
attitude toward Sally. Comparison with melodramatic actress
Sarah Bernhardt and the eternally innocent Mary Pickford
(once known as America's Sweetheart) implies the woman
might be exaggerating, but she puts on a good show and is
both touching and likeable.

The true horrors—that she was beaten, robbed, mugged,
stabbed—are given short shrift, as if the author does not
quite believe them. Instead, the author lingers on the cockroach story, describes it as the real "experience of unrelieved horror"—and makes sure we learn of Sally's happy
ending to that incident. Even Sally's obsessive lament in
life—"What She Has Suffered"—becomes like a headline
on a Broadway marquee by the simple device of capitaliz-
ing it.

The author's voice, achieved through using all the above
techniques, tells us to be fond of Sally but to not take her too
seriously. The author's skill with language makes us smile
down on Sally with comfortable condescension.

Or take the story on the next page. On the surface, this
is a description of an annual agricultural fair in Massachusetts.
The writer is describing two booths at the fair: one run by a

group that is opposed to legal abortions, and, across the aisle, another run by a cosmetic company:

> "When do you decide to throw a baby out?" a woman asks the crowd. "This is human life we're talking about." She wore her moral vigilance under a lightly frosted pixie cut, and the Mary Kay Cosmetics representative across the aisle would like to do something about both. Her displeasure shows when the anti-abortion harangues interrupt a client consultation. Lipstick cocked at the face of a milky housewife, she presses her eyes tight and steeples her brows, pausing until the worst is over.
> "Abortion . . ."
> "I think this is your . . ."
> "is a crime . . ."
> "color. Let me show you the . . ."
> "against nature."
> "polish to match."
> Over the course of a week at the large fairgrounds, an hour and a half north of Boston, there will be shearing, exhibitions of pulling horses and donkeys, public milking contests, beauty contests for cows and for women, fiddling duels, and greased-pole climbing.[2]

Under the "facts," the author has taken pains to ridicule in several effective ways the woman who is against legal abortion:

- He trivializes her beliefs by implying they are something she wears on the surface, a mere cosmetic gloss, like her "lightly frosted pixie cut."
- He juxtaposes her commentary with makeup advice. By focusing equally on abortion issues and makeup advice, he puts them on the same plane.
- He attributes to the cosmetic saleswoman negative reactions that the writer himself clearly feels (she feels "displeasure" at the "harangues"), and he describes in detail her pained expression (with "lipstick cocked"—like a trigger, perhaps?).

- He then moves on to the other events at the fair—"public milking contests, beauty contests for cows and for women." By juxtaposing "beauty contests for cows and women," he again brings two disparate events down to one common plane, and so mocks Miss America–type contests. He also leaves the impression that this antiabortionist is just part of the smorgasbord of fun.

The author has arranged his facts and observations to establish voice. By putting two disparate conversations side by side, he conveys his own point of view to the reader.

Before we ponder whether or not it is "fair" for him to do this, consider this third example.

On the surface, it, too, is a straightforward story about a benefit for the Municipal Art Society, with Jacqueline Kennedy Onassis as one of the organizers.

She has become the [Municipal Art] society's lure, the presence the press always reports. She co-chaired its dinner in a tent at the Isamu Noguchi Garden Museum in Long Island City, Queens. The evening was instructive . . .

As usual, she was the cynosure of all eyes. "The museum is so fresh, so real, so marvelous," she told Mr. [Philip] Johnson. They are dear friends. They agreed that the naked gray tent hung with nothing but Noguchi lamps was spectacular.

Around them, guests craned to get a look. Walters hovered. A tycoon whom Mr. Johnson knew came by and wangled an introduction. Afterward, she took out her glasses to read the program. She wore black pants and a beaded gunmetal satin jacket. Her enormous earrings were rhinestone. Her bracelet was diamonds.

A breeze set the Noguchi lamps to swaying. Mr. Johnson was entranced. Mrs. Onassis was entranced. Mr. Noguchi looked up approvingly. Miss DeCuevas and Mr. Walton were deep in conversation. Miss Graham hadn't a clue . . .

The Japanese Ambassador and his wife joined her table. He was transfixed. She pulled out a cigarette, lighted it and one of her giant earrings fell off.

She pushed back her chair. Mr. Johnson pushed back his chair. He crawled around and finally found it in pieces. "Somebody would think you dropped it to spice up the party," he said.

Mrs. Onassis studied her broken earring. Waiters studied her studying. The Japanese Ambassador looked confused. It was explained to him that New York parties were so noisy talk was impossible. He may not have heard.

Mrs. Onassis smiled. Mr. Johnson stared at bits of carrot and gravy congealing on his plate. The speaker droned on, pronouncing city officials "more interesting than others in the world—of course I don't know Paris" and slipped the Statue of Liberty into his finale.

Others spoke. Dessert arrived. Pols worked the room. But the photographers massed to shoot Mrs. Onassis again and again. And at long last, she got up, walked among the tables and delivered her tribute and the society's medal to Mr. Noguchi.

Another must-attend gathering was history. And on her way out, strangers reached out to touch her and tell her how wonderful she had been.[3]

Just under the skin of this story, the author is delivering her jabs. Repeated use of short sentences and paragraphs gives a stilted, artificial feeling to the event. The people seem to move like mannequins: they arrive; they smile; they wave; they push back their chairs; they stare at their jewelry and food and each other. The few quotes are trivial, implying that the speakers are trivial. Because of the writing style, it appears to be a story about disconnection and disengagement, high on style, low on substance.

Is it fair? Your response to the writing in each of the three above examples depends on your feelings about each subject: if you are working for the rights of the homeless, if you are against legal abortion, if you are a fan of Jackie Onassis—you might be annoyed or even angry.

If, on the other hand, you have little sympathy for the poor and displaced, if you are pro-choice and believe in the right to legal abortion, if you get a kick out of ribbing the rich-and-famous—then these stories might make you smile.

Whatever your response, remember that the feature is intrinsically subjective, not objective. This makes it radically different from the standard hard-news story, in which the opinion and reaction of the author are supposed to be subordinated to the news itself. In theory, a hard-news reporter should not let his or her personal views influence how the story is written; in reality, of course, it is almost impossible to be so objective as to be invisible in the story. However, hard-news reporters are mandated to keep their views in the background, and to try to be fair.

The feature writer has no such mandate. The feature is not obligated to present all points of view. It is not obligated to be evenhanded. In fact, the most successful feature writers in this century were and are, in many cases, the most opinionated: A. J. Liebling, Tom Wolfe, Joan Didion, Lillian Ross, Hunter Thompson, Norman Mailer. While they may seldom use the personal pronoun "I" in their nonfiction writing, each writer's voice lies just below the surface of the story, molding it to fit the writer's interpretation of events.

This is not to say that the feature writer should not tell the truth: as with hard news, quotes must be accurate and not twisted out of context; description must describe reality, not fantasy; and the writer has an obligation to reflect with some degree of precision the scenario, the personality, or the controversy at hand. But, given all that, the writer has enormous scope to shape the story to reflect his or her personal view of the world.

In this sense, the feature writer is manipulative and controlling. The characteristics that psychoanalysts tell us are harmful to personal relationships work to our advantage when we commit the act of writing. As Joan Didion says:

> In many ways writing is the act of saying I—of imposing oneself upon other people, of saying listen to me, see it my way, change your mind. It's an aggressive, even a hostile act. You

can disguise its aggressiveness all you want with veils of subordinate clauses and qualifiers and tentative subjunctives, with ellipses and evasions—with the whole manner of intimating rather than claiming, of alluding rather than stating—but there's no getting around the fact that setting words on paper is the tactic of a secret bully, an invasion, an imposition of the writer's sensibility on the reader's most private space.[4]

With newsprint as a shield between them and their projected opinions, writers can bully, ridicule, praise, or pity. But your point of view must have a ring of truth. "The most essential gift for a good writer is a built-in, shock-proof shit detector. This is the writer's radar and all great writers have had it," said Ernest Hemingway, who began his career as a newspaper reporter.

Younger feature writers often produce copy known for its bite, its edge, and its rather merciless gaze on all that is unfair, unjust, immoral, and just plain stupid in the world.

Older feature writers (say, over 35) who stay in nonfiction writing (some move into fiction, some become editors, some educators) and who have retained a purity of vision (many, alas, lose it along the way) have a shot at becoming great writers. Their bite may be more subtle, but with the weight of years it will be deeper. "You develop a consciousness as you grow older which enables you to write about anything, in effect, and write about it well," says Norman Mailer. "That is, provided you keep your consciousness in shape and don't relax into the flabby styles of thought which surround one everywhere."[5] Their good instincts are reinforced by the extra years of just plain living through the complexities of their own personal experiences. And their prose improves with all that practice.

Tom Wolfe is one writer, for instance, who has improved with age. His early work in the 1960s—outrageous for its day in both style and content—charted a new terrain of possibility for nonfiction. But in one sense, that early work did not hold up to the test of time: today's students find it hyperbolic and egocentric and complain that the style interferes with the substance. (They are missing the point, of course, that for Wolfe the medium often *was* the message.) But Wolfe hasn't stopped growing. In his later work in the 1970s, the glare has been polished to a deeper sheen. In *The Right Stuff,* for instance, his book about the early days of the U.S. space program, his voice became more forgiving of human foible, without losing its ability to zap and tweak the ludicrous, the inane, the ritualistic and banal.

But with this kind of freedom to intrude upon your story comes a responsibility to be aware of the point of view you wish to convey. When you sit down to write, you should already know how you feel about the subject at hand. If not, then you should be aware that you are still sliding around in search of a point of view, and when you find it in the course of writing, you may need to alter parts of the story to fit it, or show clearly within the story itself how or why your point of view has changed. When writing, ask yourself: How do I feel? Why do I feel that way? Is it justified, or should I be suspicious of my reaction? How am I going to convey my point of view in my story? Can I justify this reaction, without getting defensive, if called upon to do so by my editor, my reader, or the people in the story? Am I willing to reevaluate my point of view?

The worst thing a writer can do is to shift his or her point of view in a story without due warning. This befuddles the reader, who feels led first in one direction, then another direction, and finally astray. Whatever ambiguities you feel when writing a story (and there will always be some) must be sorted out in your own mind. And if expressed in the story, they must be handled clearly and carefully, so the reader has clear signposts along the way. Otherwise, the reader comes to the inevitable conclusion that the writer is incompetent at best, an idiot at worse.

What happens when a writer loses his or her voice?

A few years ago, the Sunday magazine of a major newspaper featured a story on Dawn Langley Simmons, a transsexual (man into woman) who shocked Charleston, South Carolina, with both her sex change operation and then her interracial marriage. In the lead, the author tells us that Ms. Simmons is now divorced, and has subsequently become engaged to another man—a felon convicted of committing three murders and a rape, among other crimes.

The author at first seems sympathetic: Ms. Simmons, while quite a character, is made to sound feisty and strong, bright and credible, a person who has overcome enormous odds to find happiness.

The author carefully catalogs Ms. Simmons's woes: illegitimate, a genital deformity, rejected by "well-bred" families.

Her first husband robbed her, trading "her Chippendale desks for $10 bills." She plunged into poverty, went on welfare, reverted from successful biographer (profiles of Jackie Kennedy and Princess Margaret, among others) to a failed writer.

Still empathetic, the author points out:

> She was a more successful man than woman, almost as though she defined woman as victim and proceeded to fit the definition. As a woman she lost the fortune the man had inherited from a distant relative on his mother's side. As a man, Gordon was a prolific and successful author; as a woman, Dawn struggled.

But, midway through the article, the author shifts her point of view, and the article becomes one of ridicule. It turns out that Ms. Simmons is probably not divorced from her first husband; that she insists she gave birth to a girl whom she calls her daughter, but she won't produce a birth certificate; that she is probably not engaged to her rapist boyfriend and when she visits him in prison, he spends most of his time ignoring her "and she ignores the fact that she is ignored."

She now lives in squalor—described in detail by the author—in upstate New York. Her daughter, 13, sleeps in filth.

> In the child's room are no lights. . . . A torn-open mattress disgorging its stuffings, naked of sheets. An awful stench of animal droppings. Upon the bed are three large dogs. . . . On the floor are newspapers soaked with the leavings of dogs.

Then, after this distasteful information, the author does another about-face. Although Ms. Simmons now is made to seem like a loser and a liar, not to mention a lousy housekeeper, the author suddenly ends on a note of praise.

> Inside this strangely draped figure, is a lovely delicacy of mind. And there is delicacy at [Ms. Simmons's] home, too, a home that lacks enough electricity, heat, and even food, a squalid place, really, but a place that has a dignity about it, the same dignity that Dawn Simmons retains in spite of her misfortunes. She manages always to be broke but not poor. In the most unnatural life she has made for herself, with its postures, excesses and contradictions, one strange fact seems to ring the most true: She is a Lady.

The reader is left not only at a loss about what is really going on here, but also with feelings of frustration (or ridicule, depending on your proclivity) aimed at the author. Nasty questions nibble at the reader's mind. Where is the delicacy of mind in this woman who loves a rapist who ignores her? Where is the dignity in the squalor? What is ladylike about being a victim? Did we miss something here?

The author missed something—in fact, quite a few things. She simply could not seem to take the story in hand, come to terms with her own ambiguities about the subject, and then convey them in a way that didn't make the reader feel jerked about like a marionette. Some of the problems in the above story could have been solved if the author had effectively *showed*—through description, anecdotes, or quotes—the dignity, the delicacy of mind, the "ladylike" qualities of the subject, instead of just *telling* the readers they are there, somewhere—if indeed they are. She didn't take advantage of the linguistic tools at her disposal.

How do you keep your words—and your story—firmly under your control? It is not easy. The "rules" of language are shifting and malleable rules, made to be bent or broken, rules that we mold and transform through use, through neglect, through serendipity. It is now possible, for example, to split an infinitive, or end a sentence with a preposition, and still be considered literate. By language I mean both basic grammar and syntax—the way words are put together in a sentence, the way the sentence is placed in the paragraph, the paragraph in the story. Didion comments on the difficulties and dynamics of language when she says:

> All I know about grammar is its infinite power. To shift the structure of a sentence alters the meaning of that sentence, as definitely and inflexibly as the position of a camera alters the meaning of the object photographed. Many people know about camera angles now, but not so many know about sentences. The arrangement of the words matters, and the arrangement you want can be found in the picture in your mind. The picture dictates the arrangement. The picture dictates whether this will be a sentence with or without clauses, a sentence that ends hard or a dying-fall sentence, long or short, active or passive. The picture tells you how to arrange the words and the arrangement of the words tells you, or tells me, what's going on in the picture.[6]

Didion's "pictures in your mind" is your voice, your point of view, that will determine how you shape your story.

Take this simple sentence: I love only you. Then note how it changes its meaning when one word—"only"—is rearranged:

I only love you.

I love you only.

Only I love you.

Every minor change in a sentence carries with it this potential for shifts of meaning, slight or dramatic. Watch for them. Watch out for them.

Here are a few guidelines concerning voice and language.

Aim to Write One Sentence You Love in Every Story

Here are a few good tries from recent stories.

On urban litterbugs:

Some of them crumple their litter and drop it stealthily, others do it as an act of defiance, while still others toss it as innocently as a flower girl tosses rose petals at a wedding.[7]

On the furnishings in a mental hospital lounge:

The decor is tight budget. Furniture is covered in vinyl and burns from cigarettes that missed the plastic ashtrays. Draperies sometimes sag as if they have seen too much.[8]

On the gentrification of Melrose Avenue in Los Angeles:

Nearby are stores named Wacko, Mad Man and Retail Slut, and newer stores with sophisticated European names like Grau and Skul, trying to outdo each other with wild new uses for punctuation, placing umlauts where accents have never gone before.[9]

On a rodeo:

It was sunny in Cheyenne, and fat clouds whitened a hard, large sky.[10]

On the Cambria Bar and Brill in Cambria, Minnesota:

But the name fits this place, a no-nonsense waystation where Yuppie-ism has yet to rear its upscale head. It is a place where a fern dare not grow, and where polyester is welcome. It is a place frequented by truckers and laborers with roofing tar and road dirt on their hands. Ask these guys about art deco and they'll tell you he's someone they graduated from high school with.[11]

It takes work to have fun with the language. But with practice, these kinds of sentences will come more often.

Be on the Lookout for Fresh Metaphors or Similes

In a metaphor, a word or phrase figuratively represents something else. Often this involves personification, in which an inanimate object is given human qualities. An excellent example appears in the second excerpt on page 117: "Draperies sometimes sag as if they have seen too much."

In a simile, one thing or person is compared with someone or something else, as in: "There are those who would compare learning to drive in Manhattan with learning to swim in the killer-whale tank at Sea World."[12] But watch out! With overuse, metaphors and similes degenerate into shopworn clichés, throwaway words, and faded phrases. There are hundred of tattered clichés, all to be avoided like the plague, such as: nick of time, smell a rat, white as a sheet, work like a horse, head over heels, cold as ice, blanket of snow, clean as a whistle, busy as a bee, pearls of wisdom, and, of course, avoid like the plague.

Be on the lookout for fresh ways of phrasing:

As busy as a moth in a mitten.

As forlorn as a melting snowman.

As cool as the other side of a pillow.[13]

John McPhee, a master of the apt analogy, writes of a Georgia man who has a voice as "soft as sphagnum." (This has the added attraction of onomatopoeia: using words that reproduce the sound of the thing you are describing.) Other McPheeisms: A woman carries a dead turtle by the tail, "like a heavy suitcase with a broken strap." And the Governor's mansion is "a million-dollar neo-Palladian Xanadu, formal as a wedding cake."

Here is how he describes a crane operator as his machine bulldozes the bends in Georgia's Ogeechee River.

> With his levers, his cables, his bucket, and hook, he handled his mats and his tank and his hunks of the riverbed *as if he were dribbling a basketball through his legs and behind his back.* He was deft. He was world class. . . . He was much aware that he was being watched, and now he reached around behind him, grabbed the [tree] stump in his bucket, and *ripped it out of the earth like a molar.* He set it at Carol's feet.[14]

Beneath the careful, solid, and apparently disinterested prose, McPhee's voice rings out.

Prefer Understatement to Overstatement

Hyperbole may work in some cases, but unless you feel comfortable (and safe) following the route of exaggeration, it is better to whisper than to shout.

Three weeks after the Chernobyl nuclear accident in Russia, when the people of adjacent Poland were still understandably worried about the radioactive cloud overhead, a writer used this lead on a story about how the country was coping:

> The Polish authorities, eager to dispel lingering fears about the effects of the Soviet nuclear reactor disaster, are finding that rumor and suspicion have longer half-lives than radioactive iodine.[15]

Since the half-life of radioactive iodine is, in fact, quite a bit longer than three weeks, the lead rings a sour note—especially when the rumors are gone and the half-life ticks on.

Luckily, few writers resort to the kind of florid prose once considered the epitome of "literary reporting," such as that of Damon Runyon, a writer in the 1920s and 1930s, who was once called the best reporter in the world. In a trial he covered, a woman was accused of killing her husband by hitting him on the head with a weight while he slept, then strangling him with a picture wire. Runyon described her thus:

> The woman, in her incongruous widows' weeds, sat listening intently to the reading of her original confession to the jury, possibly the most horrible tale that ever fell from human lips, the tale of a crime unutterably brutal and cold-blooded and unspeakably dumb.

In this century, writers have learned that the best way to convey true horror is to describe it without comment, as John

Hersey did in writing about Hiroshima on August 6, 1945, the day the first atom bomb fell.

While this was one event that can be fairly described as "a crime unutterably brutal," Hersey chose not to berate the reader with hyperbole. Instead, he quietly described the lives of six ordinary people on that extraordinary day.

One of them was Mr. Tanimoto, a minister. Through his eyes, we see the suffering.

> Mr. Tanimoto, fearful for his family and church, at first ran toward them by the shortest route, along Koi Highway. He was the only person making his way into the city; he met hundreds and hundreds who were fleeing, and every one of them seemed to be hurt in some way. The eyebrows of some were burned off and skin hung from their faces and hands. Others, because of pain, held their arms up as if carrying something in both hands. Some were vomiting as they walked. Many were naked or in shreds of clothing. On some undressed bodies, the burns had made patterns—of undershirt straps and suspenders and, on the skin of some women (since white repelled the heat from the bomb and dark clothes absorbed it and conducted it to the skin), the shapes of flowers they had on their kimonos. Many, although injured themselves, supported relatives who were worse off. Almost all had their heads bowed, looked straight ahead, were silent, and showed no expression whatever.

Another witness was Dr. Sasaki:

> There were so many that [Dr. Sasaki] began to pass up the lightly wounded; he decided that all he could hope to do was to stop people from bleeding to death. Before long, patients lay and crouched on the floors of the wards and the laboratories and all the other rooms, and in the corridors, and on the stairs, and in the front hall, and under the portecochere, and on the stone front steps, and in the driveway and courtyard, and for blocks each way in the streets outside. Wounded peo-

ple supported maimed people; disfigured families leaned together. Many people were vomiting. A tremendous number of
schoolgirls—some of those who had been taken from their
classrooms to work outdoors, clearing fire lanes—crept into
the hospital. In a city of two hundred and forty-five thousand,
nearly a hundred thousand people had been killed or doomed
at one blow; a hundred thousand more were hurt.[16]

Hersey's "voice" is here, but he is not shouting. His
voice is not colorless, but, rather, relentless: it repels, yet
mesmerizes; it is awful, yet compelling. A voice that seems
disengaged, almost stunned in the telling, much like the survi-
vors themselves on that day, and for as long after as they
managed to live.

Let the Language Reflect the Subject Matter Whenever Possible

If you do this well, you can bring the reader closer to the story
and make him or her feel "inside" the subject. If you flub it,
so that your attempt at imitation seems only cute or quaint,
then you will distance the reader, who will get caught up in
your linguistic antics rather than in the story itself.

In a story about a bar in rural Georgia, one writer chose
a few colloquialisms to entice the reader.

> Patrons of the art of rhymes and rhythms drive over from
> Shellman's Bluff and St. Simons and Midway and Brunswick to
> hear him sing and to handle a few long-necked bottles of Bud.
> It ain't easy to find his place.[17]

Sometimes a quote provides the best and easiest forum
for highlighting speech patterns. When an old man in the rural
Midwest accidentally killed his own dog, the reporter let him
describe it in his own inimitable way.

"I killed him last Friday," Pete says. "Ran over him with my car. I had him out for his run and he ran right in front of me.

"Two yips and he was a goner."[18]

At its best (and you have to be at your best to do it) you can use not only words but the way the sentences are laid out on the page to reflect the subject itself. Michael Herr did this when writing about his experiences during the Vietnam War. He tried to write *inside* the rage, the exhaustion, the obscenities, the fascination with death of many of the young soldiers involved in jungle combat, as in this paragraph about coming under attack.

Pucker and submit, it's the ground. Under Fire would take you out of your head and your body, too, the space you'd seen a second ago between subject and object wasn't there any more, it banged shut in a fast wash of adrenalin. Amazing, unbelievable, guys who'd played a lot of hard sports said they'd never felt anything like it, the sudden drop and rocket rush of the hit, the reserves of adrenalin you could make available to yourself, pumping it up and putting it out until you were lost floating in it, not afraid, almost open to clear orgasmic death-by-drowning in it, actually relaxed. . . . Maybe you couldn't love the war and hate it inside the same instant, but sometimes those feelings alternated so rapidly that they spun together in a strobic wheel rolling all the way up until you were literally High On War, like it said on all the helmet covers. Coming off a jag like that could really make a mess out of you.[19]

These sentences rush by breathlessly, moved forward by run-on sentences, strung-out phrases, by allusions to sports and drugs and strobe lights and, especially, sex.

But any event, even one that is fairly routine, can lend itself to reflective language. Consider this description of the simple act of a police car pulling over on a highway.

Now, in a screech of brakes, another car came onto the scene. It went by us, then spun around with squealing tires and pulled up on the far shoulder. It was a two-tone, high-speed, dome-lighted Ford, and in it was the sheriff of Laurens County. He got out and walked toward us, all Technicolor in his uniform, legs striped like a pine-barrens tree frog's, plastic plate on his chest, name of Wade.[20]

These four sentences seem to move in much the same rhythm as the action they are describing. Let's look closely at them.

SENTENCE 1:

"Now, *in a screech of brakes,* another car came onto the scene." The sentence barely begins when it suddenly pulls itself up short, like the car, with the prepositional phrase "in a screech of brakes."

SENTENCE 2:

"It went by us, *then spun around with squealing tires* and pulled up on the far shoulder." This sentence pivots around its center, just as the car spins on the asphalt, then pulls up to a quiet ending, just as the car itself comes to a stop.

SENTENCE 3:

"It was a two-tone, high-speed, dome-lighted Ford, and in it was the sheriff of Laurens County." This sentence sashays with self-importance: a flashy self-importance in the snappy way the car is described with three quick, hyphenated adjectives; and a no-nonsense self-importance in the way its occupant is identified in the very last words. While the first two sentences were interrupted for effect, this sentence joins two independent but equally forceful clauses. It begins quietly ("It was"), crescendos to a symbol of power (the police car), begins quietly all over again ("in it was") and crescendos to another symbol of power (the sheriff himself). This is the only sentence in the paragraph to contain all description and no action, and it serves as the anchor—the base of power—for the entire paragraph. It is the sentence around which the paragraph itself pivots.

SENTENCE 4:

"He got out and walked toward us, all Technicolor in his uniform, legs striped like a pine-barrens tree frog's, plastic plate on his chest, name of Wade." This sentence moves like the event being described: all the action takes place right away in the independent clause (he got out and walked) and those waiting for him have a chance to size him up—just as we do as we read the subsequent description. "Name of Wade," saved for the last, not only reflects the way a trooper might talk ("Name's Wade") and offers some nice assonance (repetition of vowel sounds), but also introduces us to him finally, nailing down the paragraph with this last hard, sharp sound.

This kind of reflective language comes only with practice. There is no shortcut. While some writers may claim to do it by "instinct," those instincts need to be trained methodically the way a dog is trained to follow a scent. Once you have the "nose" for it, then you will know in which direction to head.

Balance Long and Short

Short sentences and paragraphs tend to grab the reader more, especially when they follow long ones. On the thirtieth birthday of Disneyland, one writer chronicled the ups and downs of the amusement park with this lead:

> Thirty years ago today, on the broad oval of Southern California farm land that his bulldozers had cleared from the orange groves, Walter Elias Disney stepped up to a microphone to

inaugurate an amusement park quite unlike anything anybody had ever seen before. Children would fly in this place, and cruise jungle rivers, and touch beaming cartoon creatures who had walked off the movie screens; winged galleons would sail them over London at midnight, thundering rockets would carry them to the moon, and whole freeways would fill with honking traffic, scaled precisely to their size. The streets would shine like polished nickels. Everyone in uniform would smile. "To all who come to this happy place," Disney said, gazing around him at the 30,000 people who had stormed Orange County to open his celebrated new park, "welcome."

They had a terrible time.[21]

The writer begins with two long graceful sentences that outline one man's dream. She follows them with two short sentences about the pragmatic aspects of that dream—streets would shine; employees would smile. This helps emphasize the dreamlike quality of the first two sentences. The quote at the end of the long paragraph is interrupted as Disney views his audience. While the bulk of the quote comes first, the important word—"welcome"—is saved for last.

By isolating that one word, the writer helps throw the bleak brief message of the second paragraph—"They had a terrible time"—into stark relief. These abrupt five words bring the lengthy fantasy to a harsh end.

Avoid Writing in the First Person

Some writers and editors will disagree with this. But the problem with writing in the first person is that it tends to degenerate into too many "I's"—both in the number that actually appear on the page, and in the general sense of intrusiveness upon the reader. It is difficult to write in the first person without seeming to suffer from ego inflation. It is easy to slide into "I feel" this way and "I feel" that way without the necessary supporting information to convince the reader why he or she should feel the same. It is easy to become lazy in the first person. Some great writers do write only in the first person. When you are a great writer, you can too. But when you are beginning, don't.

Some people will disregard this advice. If you must, then at least see how few "I's" you can put in your copy. When you are done with a draft, circle your "I's," then rewrite to get rid of half of them.

Eschew Bloated or Inappropriate Words

These muffle your voice and muddy your copy. There are several kinds of linguistic traps to avoid.

Mucky Phrases that Hide More than They Reveal. A recent story on the Persian Gulf quoted a Pentagon official who said that patrol of the region was improving as "allied units practice inter-operability." Why not just say the allies are learning to work together—or some simple variation? A former governor of Florida told a reporter that the Florida courts are "following expedited procedures" to move death-row prisoners into the electric chair. Why not just say they've cut some red tape (and you'd better explain what the shortcuts are, which this story didn't). When bureaucrats commit the linguistic crime of saying such inanities, journalists should not make it worse by casting them abroad. A cleaned-up paraphrase will do.[22]

Unfortunately, jargon seems to be an inevitable by-product of today's "-ologies"—technology, sociology, psychology, and so on. Be aware that it is an insidious and ubiquitous part of our culture.

Following is a "Handy Guide to Jargon" that illustrates the possibilities.

To use it, you do not need to understand the meaning of

the words. Just choose any three-digit number, and then read across the columns. It graphically demonstrates George Orwell's contention that modern writing at its worst "consists in gumming together long strips of words which have already been set in order by someone else, and making the results presentable by sheer humbug. The attraction of this way of writing is that it is easy. . . . If you use ready-made phrases, you not only don't have to hunt about for words, you also don't have to bother with the rhythms of your sentences, since these phrases are generally so arranged as to be more or less euphonious."[23]

You can create impressive and intimidating phrases such as "integrated digital concept" and "responsive monitored contingency."

Handy Guide to Jargon[24]

0. integrated	0. management	0. options
1. total	1. organizational	1. flexibility
2. systematized	2. monitored	2. capability
3. parallel	3. reciprocal	3. mobility
4. functional	4. digital	4. programming
5. responsive	5. logistical	5. concept
6. optional	6. transitional	6. time-phase
7. synchronized	7. incremental	7. projection
8. compatible	8. third-generation	8. hardware
9. balanced	9. policy	9. contingency

Redundancies. Out of habit, people tend to be unnecessarily repetitive when speaking. However, it is crucial to be concise when writing. Watch out for phrases like these:[25]

owned his own home	owned his home
Jewish rabbi	rabbi

8 P.M. tonight	8 P.M. *or* 8 tonight
during the winter months	during the winter
burned in the flames	burned
evacuate residents from their homes	evacuate
smothered to death	smothered
strangled to death	strangled
temporary reprieve	reprieve
temporary stay of execution	stay of execution
a great future ahead of him	a great future
won a victory	won
tuition fees	tuition
new breakthrough	breakthrough
multipart series	series
unite together	unite
racial apartheid	apartheid
revert back	revert
consensus of opinion	consensus
old adage	adage

Commonly Misused Words and Malapropisms.   Lots of English words sound similar but have meanings that differ slightly or dramatically. These include words such as affect/effect; allude/elude; averse/adverse; equable/equitable.

A host of other English words sound different from one another, but seem so similar in meaning that one is inadvertently used in the other's place. These include: compose/comprise; imply/infer; less/fewer; oral/verbal.

When a word seems slippery, double-check its meaning in the dictionary.

The humorous misuse of a word is called a malapropism. You commit a malapropism when you use a word that sounds similar to another word, but is an inappropriate substitution, as in "The ships buttoned down their hatches" (instead of battened them down), or "it works for all intensive purposes" (instead of for all intents and purposes).

Malapropisms are most delicious when committed by

someone else. While they are often funny to read and hear, don't use them through neglect. Paula LaRocque, assistant managing editor and writing coach for the *Dallas Morning News,* recalls a character from her childhood who said he never married because he didn't want "a grindstone around his neck," who believed that "too many cooks boil the broth," and who said that plenty of immigrants came to America because they heard that everything was "paid in gold" and as a result found themselves in a "melting pot of duck soup."[26]

Linguist Jacques Barzun recalls a Houston Oilers coach known for such malapropisms as "This is the crutch of the problem" (crux), "We're changing our floormat" (format), and "He has a chronicle knee injury" (chronic). A few other classics from Barzun's *Simple and Direct* include:

> Both operations were performed by the illusory Dr. B. in California. [elusive]
>
> I fell for him at once—his looks, his manners: he was the perfect antithesis of a gentleman. [epitome, no doubt]
>
> The suggestion was greeted with overweening disapproval. [overwhelming][27]

Turn to your dictionary not only when in doubt. Use it to double-check those words you are sure you know the meaning of—or do you?[28]

❏ VOICE EXERCISES

1. Find a newspaper or magazine feature article that you feel contains a definite point of view even though it is not written in the first person.

- What is the writer's point of view toward the subject?
- How is that point of view conveyed?

- Are there any "hidden" messages behind the quotes used in the story? What are they?
- Does the writer use colloquialisms? If so, where? Do they help or hurt the story?
- Pick out one of the descriptions in the story. Is the writer conveying any hidden messages through what is included or omitted? What are those messages?
- Does the writer's voice at any point become too intrusive? Where? What is he/she doing that bothers you?
- What techniques does he/she use that you would imitate?

2. Be aware of verbose writing.

A. Rewrite this bad writing in as few words as possible.

The time taken to fall asleep in healthy males and females of all ages averages about twenty minutes. Waking should occur spontaneously. The need for an artificial awakening device indicates that there has been insufficient sleep, and the individual will suffer for it with reduced alertness during the waking period that follows.[29]

B. Rewrite this good writing from the Old Testament (Ecclesiastes) into bad modern English.

I returned, and saw under the sun, that the race is not to the swift, nor the battle to the strong, neither yet bread to the wise, nor yet riches to men of understanding, nor yet favour to men of skill; but time and chance happeneth to them all.[30]

3. How tight are your sentences? How good is your grammar?

A. Cut unnecessary words from these expressions:
- throughout the entire night
- currently serving a 20-year sentence
- gave birth to a little baby girl

- set an all-time school record
- owns a private beach
- an autopsy to determine the cause of death
- at the corner of Mercer and Bleecker streets
- the fact that she had been warned
- will revert back in 100 years
- four complimentary passes
- the other alternative
- the incumbent senator
- was totally destroyed
- an annual meeting every year
- elected by an overwhelming landslide vote

B. Many (or perhaps all) of these words contain spelling errors. Correct as necessary.[31]

seperation	aquit
accomodate	alot (many)
occasion	predominately
publicly	withheld
embarass	occurred
subpoena	alchoholic
wierd	reccommend
achieve	flourescent
alright	drunkeness
ecstacy	transend
suprise	judgment
reknowned	maintainance
ommission	homicide
agression	licence
excercise	mispell
pasttime	newstand
parrallel	bookeeper
neccessary	Carribean
desperate	similiar
committment	tyrrany

C. Correct the errors in the following sentences:

1. Winning the lottery had a significant affect on her life.
2. I am adverse to anything that seems unethical.

3. The city is composed of the very rich and the very poor.
4. He is different than his father.
5. There were cushions on either side of the couch.
6. The body laid in state for two days.
7. She made a verbal promise.
8. Over 10,000 fans cheered the Rangers.
9. It's the principal of the thing.
10. Although they urged him to speak, he was reluctant.
11. The teacher refuted the child's claims.
12. She never knew who's fault it was.
13. Now, he had less reasons to be optimistic.
14. Hopefully, the hottest days are past.
15. She alluded the robber.

To check your answers to this exercise, refer to the guide on the following pages, from the Associated Press Managing Editor Association Writing and Editing Committee's list of "Fifty Common Errors in Newspaper Writing."[32]

Affect, effect. Generally, *affect* is the verb; *effect* is the noun. "The letter did not *affect* the outcome." "The letter had a significant *effect*." BUT *effect* is also a verb meaning *to bring about.* Thus: "It is almost impossible to *effect* change."

Allude, elude. You *allude* to (or mention) a book. You *elude* (or escape) a pursuer.

Annual. Don't use *first* with it. If it's the first time, it can't be annual.

Averse, adverse. If you don't like something, you are *averse* (or opposed) to it. *Adverse* is an adjective: *adverse* (bad) weather, *adverse* conditions.

Compose, comprise. Remember that the parts *compose* the whole and the whole is *comprised* of the parts. You *compose* things by putting them together. Once the parts are put together, the object *comprises* or is *comprised* of the parts.

Demolish, destroy. They mean to do away with *completely*. You can't partially demolish or destroy something, nor is there any need to say *totally* destroyed.

Different from. Things and people are different *from* each other. Don't write that they are different *than* each other.

Drown. Don't say someone was *drowned* unless an assailant held the victim's head under water. Just say the victim *drowned.*

Ecology, environment. They are not synonymous. *Ecology* is the study of the relationship between organisms and their *environment.*

> Right: The laboratory is studying the *ecology* of man and the desert.
> Right: There is much interest in animal *ecology* these days.
> Wrong: Even so simple an undertaking as maintaining a lawn affects *ecology.*
> Right: Even so simple an undertaking as maintaining a lawn affects our *environment.*

Either. It means one or the other, not both.

> Wrong: There were lions on *either* side of the door.
> Right: There were lions on *each* side of the door.

Flout, flaunt. They aren't the same words; they mean completely different things and they're very commonly confused. *Flout* means to mock, to scoff, or to show disdain for. *Flaunt* means to display ostentatiously.

Funeral service. A redundant expression. A funeral *is* a service.

Head up. People don't *head up* committees. They *head* them.

Hopefully. One of the most commonly misused words, in spite of what the dictionary may say. *Hopefully* should describe the way the subject *feels.* For instance: Hopefully, I shall present the plan to the president. (This means I will be hopeful when I do it.) But it is something else again when you attribute hope to a nonperson. You might write: Hopefully, the war will end soon. This means you hope the war will end soon, but it is not what you are writing. What you mean is: I hope the war will end soon.

Imply, infer. The speaker implies. The hearer infers.

Lay, lie. *Lay* is the action word; *lie* is the state of being.

Wrong: The body will *lay* in state until Wednesday.
Right:　　The body will *lie* in state until Wednesday.
Right:　　The prosecutor tried to *lay* the blame on him.

However, the past tense of *lie* is *lay*.

Right:　　The body *lay* in state from Tuesday until Wednesday.
Wrong: The body *laid* in state from Tuesday until Wednesday.

The past participle and the plain past tense of *lay* is *laid*.

Right:　　He *laid* the pencil on the pad.
Right:　　He *had laid* the pencil on the pad.
Right:　　The hen *laid* an egg.

Leave, let: *Leave alone* means to depart from or cause to be in solitude. *Let alone* means to be undisturbed.

Wrong: The man had pulled a gun on her but Mr. Jones intervened and talked him into *leaving her alone*.
Right:　　The man had pulled a gun on her but Mr. Jones intervened and talked him into *letting her alone*.
Right:　　When I entered the room I saw that Jim and Mary were sleeping so I decided to *leave them alone*.

Less, fewer. If you can separate items in the quantities being compared, use *fewer*. If not, use *less*.

Wrong: The Rams are inferior to the Vikings because they have *less* good linemen.
Right:　　The Rams are inferior to the Vikings because they have *fewer* good linemen.
Right:　　The Rams are inferior to the Vikings because they have *less* experience.

Like, as. Don't use *like* for *as* or *as if*. In general, use *like* to compare with nouns and pronouns; use *as* when comparing with phrases and clauses that contain a verb.

> Wrong: Jim blocks the linebacker *like* he should.
> Right:　Jim blocks the linebacker *as* he should.
> Right:　Jim blocks *like* a pro.

Oral, verbal. Use *oral* when use of the mouth is central to the thought; the word emphasizes the idea of human utterance. *Verbal* may apply to spoken or written words; it connotes the process of reducing ideas to writing. Usually, it's a *verbal* contract, not an *oral* one, if it's in writing.

Over, more than. They aren't interchangeable. *Over* refers to spatial relationships: The plane flew over the city. *More than* is used with figures: In the crowd were more than 1,000 fans.

Principle, principal. A guiding rule or basic truth is a principle. The first, dominant, or leading thing is *principal. Principle* is a noun; *principal* may be a noun or an adjective.

> Right:　It's the *principle* of the thing.
> Right:　Liberty and justice are two *principles* on which our nation is founded.
> Right:　Hitting and fielding are the *principal* activities in baseball.
> Right:　Robert Jamieson is the school *principal.*

Refute. The word connotes success in argument and almost always implies an editorial judgment.

> Wrong: Father Bury *refuted* the arguments of the pro-abortion faction.
> Right:　With the new DNA evidence, the attorney was able to refute her client's guilt.

Reluctant, reticent. If he doesn't want to act, he is *reluctant.* If he doesn't want to speak, he is *reticent.*

That, which. *That* tends to restrict the reader's thought and direct it the way you want it to go; *which* is non-restrictive, introducing a bit of subsidiary information. For instance:

> The lawnmower that is in the garage needs sharpening. (Meaning: We have more than one lawnmower. The one in the garage needs sharpening.)

The lawnmower, which is in the garage, needs sharpening. (Meaning: Our lawnmower needs sharpening. It's in the garage.)

Note that *which* clauses take commas, signaling they are not essential to the meaning of the sentence.

Who, whom. A tough one, but generally you're safe to use *whom* to refer to someone who has been the object of an action. *Who* is the word when the somebody has been the actor:

> A 19-year-old woman, to *whom* the room was rented, left the window open.
> A 19-year-old woman, *who* rented the room, left the window open.

Who's, whose. Though it incorporates an apostrophe, *who's* is not a possessive. It's a contraction for *who is*. *Whose* is the possessive.

> Wrong: I don't know *who's* coat it is.
> Right: I don't know *whose* coat it is.
> Right: Find out *who's* there.

▫ 7 ▫

THE WEAVE

THE HARD-NEWS STORY uses the inverted pyramid form: most important information on top, least important on the bottom. The feature story, however, has no intrinsic shape. It must be pieced together like a puzzle. It must be plotted like a game of chess. This refusal to be married faithfully to one form makes the shape of the feature difficult to control: it is why some great hard-news reporters never become great, or even good, feature writers. For in addition to the "craft" of reporting, which can to a large extent be learned, it takes that added instinct for rooting out the right words with all the compulsive single-mindedness of a bee after honey. It also takes a delight in the language, a delight so strong that it compensates for the torment of wrestling with words.

However, the feature does have several *component parts* that remain the same, even though the final shape of each feature may be different. Previous chapters have addressed some of these components: the *lead* (chapter 1), *transitions* (chapter 2), *description* (chapter 4), and *quotes* (chapter 5) needed to hook them together.

There are other components as well, which will be discussed in this chapter:

1. The *Hook*
2. The *Anecdote*
3. The *Synopsis*
4. The *Portrait*
5. Boring But Important Information *(BBIs),* such as statistics
6. The *End*

These components, blended together, give body and texture to the feature. However, remember that it is the *way* they are incorporated into the story that makes them enhance or hinder the story. They should, at best, propel the story forward; at worst, they should not let it stop too long.

Writing, in general, is divided into two basic types: narration and exposition. "Narration" is the term used to describe events presented in chronological order. It is a time sequence that gives forward motion to a story. Narration implies some movement through time. Some of these components can be used as narrative devices: the *quote* or *anecdote* that tells a story; the *portrait* that recounts an event.

"Exposition" is the term used to describe the halt of a story to give it depth and breadth. *Description,* the *hook,* the *synopsis,* and Boring But Important Information (*BBIs*) such as statistics can all be used as expository devices. The challenge is to weave the narration and exposition in such a way that the story holds solidly together. If it is constructed strong and well, it will grow old gracefully.

The Hook

The hook tells the reader *what the story is about.* It is different from the lead. The lead gets the reader into the story, but does not convey the breadth and depth of the story unless the writer has resorted to a hard-news lead (see Summation, page 22).

Generally, however, the feature lead is not expected to say what the story is about. Its primary function is to lure the reader *into* the story. Because of this, at some point early in the story, the writer must figuratively stand back, take the reader by the hand, and say: "Now, dear reader, I am going to tell you the gist of this story." This is the hook. In shorter features (1,000–1,500 words) the hook may appear within the first paragraph. In longer, magazine-length features, it may appear several paragraphs into the story. By this time, the reader is usually engaged enough in the story to keep on reading.

The hook should be clear, simple, to the point. While you may not want to reveal *all* (you may, for instance, want to hold in reserve a surprise twist for near the end) you must reveal enough to be fair to the story.

The hook is the only place in the story where you have an *obligation* to intrude deliberately on the story and inform the reader of what is to come.

For example, an article on the problem of getting medical help in the Arctic leads with three anecdotes about people who were severely ill. Then, in the fourth paragraph, the writer steps back to say what the story is about.

Here is the hook:

Emergency medical flights, a few of which receive prominence in world headlines as "mercy flights," are commonplace in the far north. They are always expensive and almost always hazardous.[1]

The writer then goes on to talk about the medical personnel, the pilots, the costs and dangers of the flights, and the kinds of medical and psychological problems endemic to the Arctic.

Depending on your subject, a hook need be only a few words long. Here is the lead *and* hook on a new political appointment:

> After only a few hours on the job yesterday, the new warden of the Bronx Men's House of Detention had been blown a kiss by one inmate and been called "beautiful" by another. [lead]
> But Gloria Viola Lee, who on Monday became the first woman in the city's history to head a men's prison [hook], made it clear very quickly that such endearments did not matter one way or another as far as running her prison was concerned.[2]

The rest of the story is about Ms. Lee's professional background, her attitude toward her new job, and other inmates' reactions.

When writing your hook, don't present too many facts too soon. You can save some basic information—especially statistics and background—for later in the story. If you reveal all your hand at the start, it may slow down entry into the story and undermine the motivation to read to the end. However, if you withhold too much for too long, you will also lose the reader, who will quickly begin to wonder what the story is about.

There is no formula for how much to put in the hook: use common sense and follow your instincts, which will improve with practice.

The Anecdote

The anecdote is a re-creation of an event, an incident, or an interaction that may include description, quotes, and background. It usually (but not always) involves a dynamic between two or more people that can be used to illustrate a point in the story—a mood, a predicament, a dilemma, a person's beliefs or experiences. It can range from a sentence to several paragraphs.

The great attraction of anecdotes is that by re-creating an event they move the story forward through time; they tell "mini-stories" within the larger story, which helps keep it moving along.

Many beginning writers tend to overlook anecdotes when they sit down to write, either because they haven't gathered enough detail to develop a good anecdote, or because they don't yet have the patience or skills to shape the anecdote in a way that will fit smoothly into the story. Anecdotes are hard to develop and present well, but they are worth the effort.

For example, the psychic scars inflicted by two drug addicts are captured in one-line anecdotes.

One addict is the mother of a 1-year-old child. While a sister is trying to get custody, the child, increasingly passive and withdrawn, continues to live with her mother. The writer uses an anecdote to convey the impact of this addiction on the child.

> When her mother drifted off into a narcotic haze, Jennifer would crawl into her lap and sit there for hours, as if to protect her.[3]

The other addict, a young man, is first described this way by the writer:

> He had always considered himself something of a physical specimen. Lean and blond, just over six feet tall, he pumped iron and practiced a strict regimen of karate throughout adolescence. That was the old Robert Black.

Then, the writer gives an anecdote:

The new Robert Black was so debilitated by heroin that when he wrestled with his mother over a syringe she found under a sofa in her apartment, he lost.[4]

Anecdotes can also be powerful metaphors. In this story about the decay of Greece's Acropolis from pollution, the writer uses a seven-sentence anecdote about one elderly tourist from Worcester, Massachusetts, to convey the mortality of men and monuments. The writer describes the ailing man's last visit to the Parthenon.

He told the taxi driver to wait for him. As he started up the path, he reflected that the Acropolis might be mortal after all. When the doctors told him last August that he had cancer and probably would not live past January, he had wrestled with his faith and come to terms with his own mortality. But, having survived his deadline, he decided to take advantage of the extra days to photograph the Parthenon one more time. He had earned his living as a photographer and had photographed it on many previous visits in all kinds of light and weather.
But as he struggled up the incline toward the Acropolis, he realized that he did not have the strength to complete the climb. He turned back toward the taxi, and when he finally got his breath, he remarked to the driver, "It's probably better to remember it as it was."[5]

This anecdote raises some questions: How did the writer happen to be there when this man got out of his taxi? How did he know what he was thinking as he walked up to the Parthenon? Perhaps he was a friend, or acquaintance. Perhaps they shared the taxi, or just happened to arrive at the same time. Perhaps this man confided his history and his fears to the writer before the visit, or after. Or perhaps the writer had to pry them out of him through cautious questioning.

Anecdotes are elusive: you must find them; they won't rush to you. The point is that the writer recognized the possibilities intrinsic in the situation; he saw the juncture between two seemingly disparate subjects—the slow death of a human being and a building—and used it.

Good anecdotes take good timing, good reporting, good instincts, and patience. They do not spring out at you; instead, you usually have to eke them out from the bits and pieces of your story. And you have to know them when you see them. In the Parthenon story, the writer's antennae were scanning for signals, for symbols of the moment—and they found one.

The Synopsis

The synopsis is a condensation of a controversy, a viewpoint, a background report on a public or private event. In a complex story, condensation of lengthy information becomes essential.

A background in hard-news reporting often helps here. After researching a story, the writer should be awash in information. It has usually come in dribs and drabs, unclear, incomplete, often redundant, sometimes superfluous, exaggerated, or misleading. It is the writer's job to sift and winnow it, and then compress it into some palatable shape—the briefer the better—that the reader can swallow painlessly. The longer the feature, the more often a writer will have to stop the story for a synopsis.

Synopses are especially useful if the story contains any of the following:

Controversy. Opposing views should be presented quickly, without allowing grandstanding by either side.

Here, for instance, is a synopsis of different views on the way to reduce the incidence of violent juvenile crime.

There is a disagreement about how to best deal with the problem. Police talk of harsher penalties with more incarceration

while child welfare advocates look for ways to reduce or even
end imprisonment.[6]

The writer then goes on to discuss each view in detail.

Here is a synopsis of a battle in Robeson County, North
Carolina, over construction of two toxic water-treatment
plants, one of them for radioactive waste.

> The residents contend that their area was selected for the
> plants because it has a median family income about half the
> national average and has historically wielded little political
> power, and because more than half of the people are black or
> American Indian.
>
> Spokesmen for GSX and US Ecology say the area was se-
> lected because it provided the best facilities for their plants.
> They both insist the plants pose no health threats to the area
> and categorically deny that the sites were political choices.[7]

In this example, as in the previous one, the writer then goes
on to analyze the problem in depth, but only *after* conveying
the scope of the story to come.

Public Events.   City council sessions, trials, award presenta-
tions, parent-teacher meetings, annual celebrations—all tend
to be messy from the writer's point of view. There's too much
detail, too much trivia, and too much repetition. A common
problem in covering them is that the resulting story is not tight
enough. Because the writer faces so much redundancy, the
decisions about what to put in and what to exclude become
more difficult. In covering public events, the writer must be
merciless in chopping away all nonessential information, and
must be sharp enough to find and highlight the most revealing
and pertinent facts—and nothing else.

When Atlanta committed millions of dollars to develop
the Underground Atlanta "marketplace" in the center of the
city, it was promised that at least 25 percent of the 150 busi-

nesses there would be minority-owned. Here is a summation of the subsequent meeting between the developers—the Rouse Company—and minority business people in city hall:

> To start fulfilling its promise, Rouse took part in a presentation at City Hall last week. Roughly 150 people, from gelato scoopers to body shop owners, crowded the council chambers to hear company and city officials tell what it takes to get a piece of the action.
>
> Mainly, money.
>
> More than a few faces dropped when the Rouse man started talking about investments of $50,000 to $1 million.
>
> Herman Pittman, who sells chicken wings out of a catering wagon called Uncle Herman's Cabin, says he has less than $10,000 in the bank. "Underground is fixed against the grassroots minorities," he said. "These people want such a foolproof package, they're going to end up with only the handpicked elite blacks who are tapped into the system."[8]

This is an effective synopsis for several reasons:

First, although 150 businesspeople were at the meeting, the writer conveys the *type* of small businesses represented by mentioning only *three* of them: gelato scoopers, body-shop owners, and a chicken-wing vendor. That's enough.

Second, he highlights *one* high-impact moment: the instant when the developer gave the bottom-line numbers needed to open a business. He sums up the general reaction: "more than a few faces dropped." That, again, is enough when backed up by a quote from one of those dropped faces.

And third, in the final paragraph above, he uses *one* quote (although he undoubtedly gleaned many, many more from the disappointed and outraged audience). The quote, it is safe to bet, is a pithy reflection of the way many people felt.

And last, but most important, the synopsis is well written. The two-word paragraph—"Mainly, money"—stands out from the longer paragraphs and sentences. Each sentence is important to the piece; there is no self-indulgence here.

Trial Reporting. Trial reporting calls on special skills in summarizing hours of testimony. Here is the synopsis of the lengthy trial of Dan White, the former member of the San Francisco Board of Supervisors, who in 1978 shot and killed both the mayor and a city supervisor of San Francisco.

> Here is some of what the jury learned, over the course of Dan White's trial: that in November 1978 Dan White resigned from his seat on the Board of Supervisors, recanted, asked [Mayor George] Moscone to reappoint him, and discovered through an inquiring reporter that the mayor had decided against it. They learned that on the morning of November 27, White, a former police officer and firefighter, loaded his gun, put 10 extra bullets in his pocket, had an aide drive him to City Hall, ignored the front entrance (with its large metal detector), climbed in through a basement window and went up to see the mayor.
>
> The jurors learned that White reloaded his gun after shooting Moscone, although it was not clear if he reloaded immediately, as police are said to do by training, or if it was a few moments later to prepare to shoot [Supervisor Harvey] Milk. They learned that White and Milk had developed an odd friendship at City Hall and had spoken favorably about each other, and that White was "a man I was proud to know and be associated with," according to the testimony of the police inspector who had obtained the confession from his old friend Dan White. They learned that White had been financially strapped and had felt extreme emotional pressure that one psychiatrist argued was linked to his consumption of "what we call junk food," in this instance principally Twinkies and Coca-Cola.[9]

In this synopsis, the writer chooses two tools that help her keep the story moving.

First, she uses long sentences (the first paragraph contains only two; the last paragraph, only three). The first three sentences are filled with activity and action, including the motive and the details of the first murder. Only the last two sentences pause to discuss some emotional aspects of the case—and by then, we are willing to read them.

Second, she uses parallel sentence construction. By repeating "the jurors learned that" and "they learned that," she establishes a rhythm that eases us through the prose.

Recurring Events.   Feature writers are often asked to cover parades, festivals, fund-raisers, and other events that present the special challenge of how to find something new and fresh to say about activities that are written up every year. The power of language goes a long way toward compensating for the boredom of the familiar.

Here is a synopsis of an upcoming annual Frontier Days celebration in Cheyenne, Wyoming.

> The Cheyenne townsfolk prepare 3,000 pounds of ham and more than 100,000 pancakes each year for the 30,000 people that show up. They mix the pancake batter in a cement truck and you'll have to sit on a bale of hay. But the price is right and nobody waits more than 20 minutes. Wyoming breakfasts—a shot of whiskey and a chaw of tobacco—are optional.[10]

Just a few well-chosen details—the pounds of ham; the number of pancakes; the cement truck used to mix pancake batter; the whiskey-and-tobacco breakfast (with, note, the colloquial expression "chaw of tobacco")—suffice to arouse interest.

Or, in the following example, the students at a junior high school in Manhattan compete against their teachers in their tenth annual basketball game. Here, the reasons for the game's popularity are summarized, followed by a quick synopsis of student dialogue to help illustrate the ambiance surrounding the event.

They love the game for so many reasons, among them:

• The opportunity to see teachers in shorts.

• The camaraderie of the court, which allows them to drop deference and proper titles, to wit, "Take the train, Epstein," "Get a haircut, Rudy," and the obligatory, "Nice hands, Herschkowitz," uttered only when Mr. Herskowitz has either flubbed a dribble or a basket. The students also get a lot of satisfaction out of shrieking "child abuse" when a member of their team is fouled and "police brutality" if the foul is committed by Officer Trifeletti.

• The fair exchange of criticism, mostly against Mr. Silkowitz, who, in all fairness, must be said to occasionally foul other players with impunity.

"Silkowitz is a butcher," said one student.

"He's a nice guy," said a fair-minded player.

"But he's a butcher," said a third.

"Who are you talking about, Silkowitz, right?" said someone, sticking his head into the circle by the bleachers.

"He'd probably be good at football," said one of the others.

"Part of his bad reputation is because he's assistant principal," said the fair-minded one.

"I'm known for my aggressive style," said Mr. Silkowitz in response.[11]

With synopses, writers rely on their skills as linguistic surgeons to excise the excess verbiage and get on with the story.

Personal Events. Some synopses focus on a specific, often cathartic, life event that is pivotal to a person's current goals, beliefs, or problems. They are written snapshots that reverse the adage that a picture is worth a thousand words. Instead, a dozen well-chosen words are worth a thousand pictures.

Again, the writer's challenge is to select the right moments and then re-create them in a brief, vivid way. People who are talking about special moments in their lives tend to be either verbose, or nearly inarticulate, about what happened and why it meant so much. Their memories may be hazy. They are rarely concise. It is up to the writer to condense and focus.

Here is how one writer handles the story of how a man bought the home of his dreams on the Georgia coast:

> He lives with his wife and sons in a house with a back porch that overlooks the river and marshes. There are rocking chairs and a swing on the porch. . . . The house is down a dirt road from where he grew up. He'd wanted to buy it for years.
>
> "One morning the owner called me and told me 'I've been saved' and that he was going to Shreveport, Louisiana, to study evangelism. He asked me if I still wanted to buy the house," Waters said. "I said bingo, praise the Lord."
>
> He remodeled it himself, doing the carpentry and masonry with the help of an out-of-work shrimper.[12]

Here, in only two paragraphs, former millionaire Millard Fuller recalls how his wife's threat to leave him changed his life:

> Unfortunately, Fuller, always thinking of the next deal, was consumed by his work. Even when he was home, he wasn't really there—until, one day, Mrs. Fuller precipitated the key crisis in his life by confronting him with a sad fact: She was leaving him because he seemed more in love with money than his family.
>
> Always a religious man and the founder of a United Church of Christ in Montgomery, Fuller was stunned. Never one to go halfway, he sold his business, gave his money away and started over, eventually bringing his family to Sumter County, Georgia, and Koinonia, an interracial Christian farming commune founded by New Testament scholar Clarence Jordan in 1942.[13]

Or a writer may pluck from a person's past *a few* details to highlight those things that best symbolize the person in the context of the story. A small-town doctor's popularity is illuminated with two taut synopses.

> He is a doctor who knows his patients.
> He knows about Mr. Smith's allergy to penicillin and the Atlanta Braves and about his fear of not being able to keep up with the younger men on the job.
> He knows about the weak tissue around Mrs. Jones' right elbow, the weakness she has for persimmon pudding and the way she became weak-kneed when her daughter who wanted to go anywhere ran off with the man who recruited her to sell magazines.[14]

In a similarly succinct manner, the criminal record of a Detroit drug addict is described thus:

> Black made a pathetic criminal. When Redford police arrested him on a routine traffic charge March 13, 1980, they found him with a stolen credit card, which turned out to belong to a Detroit policeman. When Black smashed in a physician's car window in Southfield on January 10, 1981, and fled with the doctor's bag, he discovered after his arrest that it contained only the doctor's laundry. When Black and a friend stole a CB radio from a woman's car in September 1981, Black hung around so long that the woman had time to return and have him arrested.[15]

The Portrait

Occasionally, it is useful to run a longer profile of one person in a story, because the person epitomizes or symbolizes a theme that the writer is trying to develop.

In these cases, the writer goes in the opposite direction from synopsis: rather than condensing, he or she lingers on a person, adding detail to the sketch, forcing the reader's gaze to rest a moment longer.

A writer who wanted to show the legacy of war on the young people of northern Ireland chose to end the feature with a finely sketched portrait of a 20-year-old woman he met in a Belfast laundromat.

> She has pictures a Chicago photographer took and sent back to her. As she gets them out, the other women in the laundry watch.
>
> The photograph shows her staring out of a window with a look of desperation on her face. She is still young, not like her friend Mary Drain, and those magic pictures make her think what life would be like—as a model, say, or an actress—away from the rubble and the shooting and the insistent call of Irish nationalities.
>
> She has lost a favorite cousin to the troubles. "He was shot once in the head. They never found out who did it," she says.
>
> But what really hurts is the way her own dreams and hopes seem to be dying day by day. Since she was 8 years old, there has been nothing but the violence.
>
> "You grow immune to it. You get used to it. All you have to do is step out of the house to see it," she says.
>
> There are no opportunities for her, and no future—except a future like Mary Drain's. There will be a boy from the Clonard for a husband, some tenderness, yes, but then a life-time in near poverty—rearing children and watching her youth slip away while the marches and funerals go on.
>
> She keeps a visitor as long as she can and then stands by the door of the laundry, watching as he drives away. There is a crowd of young men outside a nearby betting shop, playing seven-card stud in the middle of a sunny morning.
>
> One calls to her, but she turns her back.[16]

The emotions and experiences of this young woman—the visit from an American who cared enough to send her pictures, her dreams of an exciting life in a safer place, the murder of her cousin, her numbness to violence, her bleak prospects for the future—these reflect, the writer feels, the emotions and experiences of the youth of northern Ireland. This is not just the story of one person: it is part of many stories, wrapped up in one.

Boring But Important Information (BBIs)

BBIs includes statistics, official reports, and background. Almost every story has some of this, and the problem is always how to fold it into the feature without coming to a dead stop. Whenever possible, weave BBIs into the middle of other, more interesting, information. Usually, the lower down in the story you put the BBIs, the better off you will be. If you have a lot of BBIs, it is usually better to scatter them throughout the story, so they don't appear as one big block of dead weight.

Statistics. Keep statistics to a minimum, as they are hard to digest. If the statistics are alarming or striking, then by all means use them but be brief and direct, as in:

> In 1986, local police charged juveniles with eight murders, 20 forcible rapes, 49 robberies, 185 aggravated assaults, 215 burglaries, 845 thefts, 136 car thefts, and 197 assaults.[17]

If you have lots of statistics, it is a good idea to build them into the infrastructure of the story. Notice how, in the following article about a bingo game in the Mashantucket Pequot Indian Reservation in Connecticut, the writer manages to personalize the statistics by blending them with the action of a "typical" day, and uses healthy verbs, most of them in the present tense, to move along the story.

> Nothing has done more for the reservation lately than bingo. The game started in July 1986 and is taking in about $10 million a year, providing about $2 million—half the tribe's income—in profit.

Every day but Tuesday and Wednesday, 800 to 1,000 people arrive here, often by chartered bus from as far as New York and Maine, and pay $25 to $150 for admission into the reservation's $4.6 million bingo hall.

There, they spend up to five hours blotting out letters and numbers on scorecards, hoping to win anywhere from $50 to $2,000 per game, and occasionally more. Much more.

Two weeks ago, Lorraine Milolinski, a housewife from Cheshire, won $22,000. "I really went bananas," she said.[18]

Nearly every sentence here is providing statistics, but they seem painless because the writer stays focused on what happens on the average day. And when he describes how much can be won, he lets a jackpot winner speak for herself. The writer could have simply written:

The reservation brings in about $2 million a year from 5-day-a-week bingo games. More than 2 million people play the game each year and the reservation has built a $4.6 million bingo hall to accommodate them. Admission is $25 to $150; players may win from $50 to $20,000 a game.

But such a paragraph is dead in the water. It is clearly better to liven it up with the techniques used in the first example.

Reports. Many stories require writers to slog through official reports and then summarize them for the reader. Usually, the briefer the summary, the better.

In a feature on a barber school, the writer sums up the course catalog in one long sentence:

The catalogue describes the exhaustive curriculum of 1,000 hours, usually accomplished over six months, which includes classes in such subjects as thinning shears, pompadours, the part, use of the towel, shaving the neck, methods of rinsing, shop ventilation, personal hygiene, shop management, first aid, and the patron-barber relationship.[19]

However, it sometimes livens up a story to have a small portion of an official report quoted verbatim. While the report may be boring as a whole, you can incorporate part of it into your story in a way that is not.

For this article on Disneyland, the writer plucked out some graphic details from the park's maintenance report:

> Park Defects Reports, issued daily for overnight repair work, July 4 and 7, partial list:
> Cigar store Indian needs touch up.
> Gate that leads to Mad Hatter does not swing back to close after opening.
> Thatching coming off roof of Mad Hatter above east door.
> All brass "Watch Your Step" signs need polish.
> Water buffalo python scene sensor not triggering—currently on override.[20]

General Background. Most stories need some background to add perspective. Background includes personal history (birthplace, parents, education, jobs) or public history (the environmental record of a corporation, the ups and downs of a school system, the track record of the last governor). Often, personal and public histories merge in a feature background.

There are three rules of thumb for inserting general background:

1. Put it in chronological order.
2. Begin it about one-third of the way into the story.
3. Keep it tight, tight, tight.

If you note the structure of most feature stories, you will see that they do adhere to these rules, simply because they work. Each of these rules, however, may be bent or broken. Since each story has its own personality, it is important to let the content guide the structure, rather than the other way around.

The End

While it is all right for a hard-news story to just drift away in
the end, the last paragraph of a feature story should be as
compelling as the first. It is important for nonfiction to have
"closure," to end as definitely as a sonnet or a play. One good
technique for closure is to make the story come full circle and
end with an echo of your lead. This kind of ending literally
"wraps up" your story by tying the end to the beginning.

For example, here is the lead and then the end to a
feature on the final destination of some of the urban poor. The
story begins:

> The man who was born in Hungary was the oldest. He had
> lived in a single-room-occupancy hotel and died in the hospital.
> He was 83 years old.
>
> The next man was 82. He lived in the same kind of hotel
> and had a sister living upstate.
>
> The third was 51 and lived in a narrow little place on the
> Bowery, with a bar on the bottom floor. His sister lived in the
> city, and came to the funeral mass. So did one of his buddies,
> who fell over in a pew, drunk, and cajoled a nun into giving
> him some spare change.
>
> The boy was 15. He was born in Bellevue Hospital, and he
> lived and died there, plagued by imaginary demons that
> seemed terribly real to him. He hanged himself with a strong
> length of cloth, and the nurses arranged to have him buried.
> He had no known relatives.
>
> None of them knew the others. Very few people still living,
> apparently, had known any of them. On a clear autumn after-
> noon, with the sky like soft-blue cotton flannel, the four of
> them were buried in the same grave, one pressed wood coffin
> atop the other.

The writer goes on to describe the cemetery for the poor
and unclaimed, run by the St. Vincent De Paul Society. After

a quote from the grave digger, the story then ends with a new litany.

> "You have four today and you might have four next week. You got to be ready for them."
>
> They were ready for them. The hole had already been dug for four more when they buried the four on that blue afternoon. And sure enough, the following week there were indeed four more.
>
> The oldest was an 88-year-old Italian immigrant who had died in a nursing home in Manhattan.
>
> The next was a 57-year-old derelict who lived in the Bowery.
>
> The third was from the Bowery, too, and was 58 years old.
>
> The fourth was a man who had lived in a tiny room on the Upper West Side and died in St. Luke's Hospital.
>
> None of them knew the others.[21]

Repetition of sentence structure (each set begins with "the oldest," "the next," "the third") and even of an entire sentence ("None of them knew the others") increases the sad sense of inevitability in this story.

Because the feature story need not follow a straight chronology from beginning to end, it is also possible to have the lead and the end reflect *the same moment in time,* with the entire story then built around that moment.

Here, for instance, is the lead on the story about the blessing of the animals for the feast of St. Francis of Assisi (also quoted in chapter 5, "Quotes").

> Dogs barked in the nave of the Cathedral of St. John the Divine on Sunday, and no one troubled to quiet them. Poodle, dachshund, Pomeranian, Labrador, and mutt, all were invited guests at an annual celebration for the feast of St. Francis of Assisi.

The writer then spends 900 words describing the animals and a few of their owners. He ends the story just as the ceremony is about to begin:

> The heavy doors opened, and the dark aisle was lit with columns of sunshine. Bits of fur blew inward. There was a hush, and a communal gasp as the elephant hove into view. Wherever you looked were humans embracing their pets, humbly expressing relationships that transcended ritual and were purely Franciscan. From the street, a lone voice carried dimly into the cathedral. "Free the elephant," howled an antivivisectionist named Teresa Rivezzo. "Set all animals free."[22]

In some dramatic cases, you can even save the "hard" news until the very end.

This story, for instance, begins with a teasing lead, an ominous prediction. Readers will not find out what happens until the final paragraph 1,000 words later.

The story begins:

> There was no warning, no way to know it was coming.
>
> It was one of those things that happens in a moment's time, shattering lives, hopes, and dreams of tomorrow.
>
> It was one of those things that can happen in any city at any time to anyone.
>
> Saturday it happened in Nashville.

The writer then describes the next ten-and-a-half hours— from 1:00 P.M. until 3:30 A.M. the following day—in the lives of two families: a 35-year-old respiratory therapist planning to drive her Camaro to a Christmas party in Nashville; and a family of four—husband and wife, both 33, with their two children, ages 9 and 5—traveling in their Datsun to their hometown in Louisiana for Christmas Day.

The story ends:

3:36 A.M. . . .
The emergency call came through on the 911 line at the Goodlettsville Police Department.

Three minutes later, Officer Terry Hutcherson pulled onto the scene.

"Everybody was dead except for the little girl," Hutcherson said. "She died a few minutes later before she ever woke up.

"It was a straight, head-on collision. The Camaro, which was on the wrong side of the interstate, ran headlong into the Datsun. The Camaro probably never had its lights on—it just slammed right into the Datsun.

"They didn't have a chance. Any of them."

Ambulances were called to collect the bodies.

Later, wreckers were called to pick up the tangled cars.

Inside the Datsun, they found suitcases, Christmas presents and toys.

In the Camaro, they found a strong smell of alcohol.[23]

However you choose to end your story, try to make the ending as strong as possible. Make it impossible for the editor to chop from the end. Make it worth reading to the very last word. Then stop.

❑ WEAVE EXERCISES

1. Clip a newspaper or a magazine feature of 2,000–3,000 words covering one of the following general areas:

- a tragedy (the aftermath of a heinous crime; promise ruined by a scandal or drugs; the death, disability, or suffering of a young person)
- light human interest (these tend to be on an unusual person or offbeat place, or on a generic topic such as selling Girl Scout cookies or treatments for baldness)

- a serious social issue (the environment, racism, crime, poverty, nuclear plants or weapons)

Now take it apart to see what makes it tick. Discuss your answers with friends or classmates.

A. Where is the hook? How deep is it inside the story? Does it work well there?

B. Does the author use anecdotes? If so, where are they? How do they add to the story?

C. What does the writer synopsize (controversy, public events, a trial, recurring events, personal events)? How tightly are the synopses written? Could any of them have been cut out without damaging the story?

D. Does the writer draw a portrait? (Does he or she focus on any particular person or event to *symbolize* the subject of the story?)

E. How are BBIs handled here? Where are statistics, reports, and general background placed in the story? Are they intrusive? If not, why not?

F. Are the lead and end both appropriate? Does the end mirror the lead? Does it "wrap up" the story in an effective way?

G. What is the author's voice here? How is it manifested?

H. Does this story move fast or slowly? Does its pacing suit the subject matter? What role do transitions play in the pacing? What role do verbs play?

I. How many quotes are used? Does each one add something important to the story? What? Could any be paraphrased?

J. Do the sentences in this story tend to be long, short, or mixed? Choose two of the paragraphs you feel are particularly well written, and find the parallel sentence structure, repetition of key words or subordinate clauses, or other literary techniques described in previous chapters.

2. Choose a second newspaper feature, vastly different in topic and tone from your choice in exercise 1.

A. Ask the same questions of this story that you asked of the previous one.
B. How do the two stories differ? How are they the same? How does the different structure reflect the difference in subject matter?
C. Which feature do you feel is better? Why?

3. Repeat the above for a feature you have written.

DOING IT

THE ACT OF WRITING begins long before you sit down in front of your typewriter or computer. Writing is, in fact, only one of several steps needed to produce a good feature article.[1] The steps are:

1. Getting the idea
2. Collecting the information
3. Clearing your mind
4. Focusing your thoughts
5. Writing
6. Editing
7. Rewriting

1. Getting the Idea

About 5 percent of my students get stuck at this stage. While most nonfiction writers are brimming with ideas, others freeze when asked to come up with them. Their minds go blank. They cannot think of a single interesting thing to write about, even in the middle of New York City.

This does not bode well for a future as a successful feature writer, for most assignments are self-generated—even those written by staff writers on newspapers and magazines. Ideas for features come from many sources, but *you* are, in effect, the primary initiator of ideas; *you* must be receptive to the story possibilities intrinsic in almost any situation. As Anna Quindlen, former columnist for the *New York Times,* explains:

> The question I am asked most often is where I come up with my ideas. The answer is that it depends on what is uppermost in the news. That is, if my car is towed, I do a column about car towing. If I have a tetanus shot, I do a column about hospital emergency rooms. If I am disgusted with the subways, I do a column on the subways. This is why I have done so many subway columns.[2]

She also just walks around the city, storing up the minutia of daily urban life, saving it for the day when it might be used in a feature.

Notice that Quindlen's definition of "the news" is "the things that happen to me." While not all feature writers have the luxury of researching and writing about what is uppermost in their minds at the moment, her basic instincts apply to all good feature writers: you find stories with which people can *identify.* You look for stories that are "hot," stories that arouse curiosity, and stories that others have overlooked. Feature writers are like perpetual students: every story is an excuse to learn about something new. To succeed, you must have the instincts of the Renaissance person: sweeping curiosity, a desire to track down answers, an enthusiasm for the unknown.

Stay tuned in to everything. If you are writing for local publications, keep your ears open for the gossip, squabbles, and changes in your neighborhood. Even if you are aiming for wider markets, neighborhood problems and concerns are often a reflection of broader regional or national events as well. Read as much as possible, and know what is being written about in newspapers (both your local paper and a larger daily) and in a range of magazines, from popular ones like *Parade* and *Redbook,* to highbrow ones like *The New Yorker* and *The Atlantic Monthly,* to specialized publications in areas that you want to write about, whether it's travel or computers or sports.

Listen to television and radio talk shows. The persons interviewed and subjects discussed can trigger ideas for other stories; they are also a fair reflection of what is considered (at least by broadcast producers) to be topical. One free-lance writer, while watching "60 Minutes" one Sunday evening, heard a U.S. senator mention that enormous amounts of tax revenues were lost to the "underground economy"—the unreported income from cash-heavy businesses. Intrigued, she called the senator's office in Washington the next morning, asked to be sent all the information he had on the subject, and used that to write a proposal for a magazine article on the underground economy. She sold it to the *New York Times Magazine.*

You need to keep your antennae up, your mind open, to catch stories before they slip away. When you find newspaper and magazine articles of interest, tear them out and save them. When you hear topics of interest on the radio or TV, write down as much identifying information as possible about the person being interviewed, as well as the name and date of the show. If you can't track down the interviewee later, you can call the producer of the show or the public-relations representative for the station, and they will often give you the phone number and address you need.

Above all, keep your eyes and ears open. Be curious. Value the incidents that happen to you, your friends, your neighbors. You never know what might spark the next story idea.

2. Collecting the Information

Depending on the nature of your story, collecting information may involve a variety of tactics: interviewing (see chapter 5, "Quotes"); footwork to track down people or to add color; on-site research of documents available only in a specific place, like a town hall or a police station. For some local stories, the collecting of information may stop here. You may have all you need to start writing.

But for all regional and national stories—and for all local stories that might have an echo in other towns or states—it is crucial that basic library research be done to find out what else has been written about the subject. You may need this background information to write a query. You will certainly need it to write your story.

Background research, which once took days or even weeks as the writer sorted through frayed, yellowed clips and dusty magazines and journals, is greatly simplified now with the use of computerized databases.

If you want to be able to do database research from home, you will need a computer, a modem, a telephone line, software that enables the computer to communicate, and a password, which you will receive when you join one of the database services.

If you do not have a computer at home, or if your home computer cannot access a database, or even if you can reach a database from home but are unsure just which retrieval system is best to use for your particular story—head for your local library.

Most librarians these days have been trained in database research, and most American and Canadian libraries can now run limited searches for you for free or a reasonable fee. If your local library is too small to offer this service, the librarians there can tell you which other libraries to call or visit for help.

Even if you are afraid of computers, know nothing about database research, and are unsure how to explain what it is you need, librarians tend to be not only patient and sympathetic enough to hear you out, but so enthusiastic about database research that they are happy to help find the best way to get the fastest answers.

About 500 databases are now available. Each one covers slightly different areas, and each one has a slightly different way of approaching the system to get information. But once you've used one, it will become easier to use others.

Information from databases comes in two basic forms: one gives you the full text; one gives you a bibliographic listing of the titles of the stories. And the research is *fast.* NEXIS (see page 167) claims that most search requests are answered in 15 to 20 seconds—which means the database can provide you with all references (but *not* the full text) to a given topic in that time. In the early stages of research, it is best to first get this bibliographic listing, then go through that list and pick out the stories you would like to see in full.

Many databases will offer a bibliography of all publications but a full text of only selected publications. (And you are more likely to get the full text of a newspaper article than of a magazine article.) Others offer *only* a bibliography, and you may then have to go into a different database to call up the whole story. When you do a bibliographic search, be sure to get a printout of the information, so you have hard copy to work with.

Once you are into a database, be sure to ask exactly the right questions, or you may find yourself swamped with too much, or irrelevant, information. This is called a "bad hit." For instance, if you are doing an article on how the strength of the dollar affects tourism in Europe, and you ask the computer to go through the data bank for every reference to *Dollar/Europe* you would probably end up with far more information than you need. If you ask the computer to search stories containing *Dollar/Europe/Tourism,* then it will limit its search to stories with all three words, and you'll probably get a "good hit."

Half a dozen databases are proving to be especially useful for nonfiction writers. Here is a list of a few of the most popular database vendors.

MEAD DATA CENTRAL

MDC is the vendor for NEXIS, sometimes called the "Cadillac" of databases. NEXIS is the largest and oldest retrieval service of full text databases, and the only one that prints the full text of the *New York Times*. Its libraries include full text articles from more than 350 newspapers, magazines, wire services, and newsletters. Besides general news, it also specializes in business and economic news. Its offerings range from Xinhua (New China News Agency) to *People* magazine to the *Congressional Record*. The main complaint for casual users is that it is more expensive to use than most other systems.

MDC also is the vendor for LEXIS, a collection of legal research databases that contain the full text of state and federal court decisions, statutes, and regulations on patents, trademarks, copyrights, tax regulations and codes, securities cases, national and international trade regulations, communications, labor laws, banking, energy and the environment, public contracts, military appeals, and many other legal areas. It also contains databases on United Kingdom and French law.

VU/TEXT

Owned by Knight-Ridder, Inc., VU/TEXT provides access to news stories and features in forty newspapers, making it the world's largest online databank of full text newspaper information. It also offers the full text of selected articles from more than 180 American and Canadian business journals; and the full text of the Associated Press and *Time, Fortune,* and *People* magazines. Reporters on the *Akron Beacon Journal,* who won the 1986 Pulitzer Prize for general news reporting for their coverage of the attempted takeover of the Akron-based Goodyear Tire and Rubber Company by a European financier, attribute their success to the use of the VU/TEXT and Disclosure databases. (Disclosure is a file of business and financial information extracted from reports that more than 12,000 public companies file with the U.S. Securities and Exchange Commission.) The Akron reporters used databases to get quick and thorough background information on both their breaking stories and "softer" profiles.

DIALOG INFORMATION SERVICES

This retrieval supermarket has more than 320 databases, most of them bibliographic listings, including extensive coverage of business, science, technical, medical, and legal news. Of particular help for feature writers are the Magazine Index and the National Newspaper Index. (These are also available on microfilm in many libraries.) The Magazine Index lists by subject matter articles, reviews, and features from more than 435 magazines. It also provides the full text of more than 100 of these magazines. The National Newspaper Index lists by subject matter stories that have appeared in the *Wall Street Journal,* the *Christian Science Monitor,* the *Los Angeles Times,* the *Washington Post,* and the *New York Times.*

DIALOG also offers NewsSearch, an index to more than 500 of the current month's trade journals, newsletters, newspapers, and magazines in the areas of health, computers, arts, law, business, education, environment, and so on. NewsSearch is updated daily, and all of the articles it indexes can be printed out in full text.

For people with home computers who don't mind searching evenings and weekends, DIALOG is one of several companies to offer a "user-friendly" retrieval system containing more than 75 databases that can be accessed for cheaper rates only at night and on weekends. Another popular, user-friendly service with low fees for evening use is After Dark, owned by BRS/SEARCH Service, which has more than 100 databases, some bibliographic, some full text.

COMPUSERVE

This company publishes *On-Line* magazine for its users and offers dozens of specialized databases. One, called NewsNet, gives access to more than 300 newsletters written by specialists in different fields, which often provide more current and valuable information on a given topic than general-interest newspapers and magazines.

COMPUSERVE and several other retrieval services (including DIALOG and NEXIS) also offer a "clipping service." If you request it, the computer will save each new story that contains the words you want (for example: *Ozone/Skin Cancer*) and the stories will be waiting for you the next time you request them.

Other useful systems include:

- WILSONLINE, which provides the computerized version of the *Reader's Guide to Periodical Literature,* as well as other indexes of periodicals on art, business, and general science.
- THE ORBIT SEARCH SERVICE, and QUESTEL, two vendors that offer a wide range of scientific, technical, and international patent information.

Database research has its price, but the price need not be high. Many public and university libraries have subsidies that allow them to do a "quick search" for you—up to about ten or twelve bibliographic citations—for free. Some may ask a nominal charge. New York University's Bobst Library, for example, charges students and faculty a $6 flat fee for a quick search with up to twelve citations, and a $12 fee for a more extensive search, plus printout charges. Find out the library's policy and estimated costs before the search, and decide what is most cost-effective for you. When you consider how long it would take you to come up with a list of even twelve background articles B.C. (Before Computers), the stained fingers from handling old clips, the strained eyes from looking at microfilm, the trips back and forth to various libraries, the cost is usually well worth it. Still, keep in mind that it may cost you $10 to have an article printed from a database, when that same article would cost you only sixty cents to photocopy.

If the expense seems prohibitive, ask the library to do only a quick bibliographic search for you, and once you have that list you can go to the back copies or microfilm section of the libary and make your own copies of the stories. This will take you longer, but your investment will be in time, not money. This is an important factor if you are doing a story on the "hope" that someone will buy it, or if expenses for an assigned story are coming out of your own pocket.

If you are planning to do database research from your home computer, you will pay for the number of minutes you are "online" (tapped into the database), plus the cost of the telephone call (most are local calls), plus the printing charges if you want a bibliography or a full text relayed to your printer. The costs, which vary according to the database you use, range from $15 to $300 an hour. Business and patent databases tend to be the most expensive. But many general databases are in the under-$60-an-hour category, and you can usually find a lot of database information and have a bibliography printed out in less than fifteen minutes: even if you're paying $60 an hour, that's still only $15.

If you are tapping into databases from home, it is recommended you buy a 1,200- to 2,400-baud modem instead of the much slower 300-baud modem, especially if you are doing a lot of full-text searching. While the retrieval service may charge you a bit more if you use this faster modem, you will be processing the information quicker—and you will still have a considerable savings. Check with the information service you wish to use and ask about its pricing structure. You can get a list of these services, with their locations and phone numbers, at your local library.

Even if you use a computer for research, you should be familiar with the basic reference books available to help you.

Many are not yet on databases. A list of the most useful reference books, plus two research exercises to help familiarize you with these books, are at the end of this chapter.

3. Clearing Your Mind

This third step of the writing process is usually called "avoidance," "writer's block," or "procrastination." You have done the research, you're ready to begin—but you find yourself thinking of reasons why you cannot. During this stage, writers appear to do anything not to write: they plant a garden, rearrange the furniture, jog, shop, sharpen pencils, fix the car, clean the closets, sleep. Every writer feels some degree of guilt about this stage, which may last half a day, or up to a month. If it lasts longer than a week or so, then it is probably no longer a "stage" in the writing process, but is more likely a case of true procrastination. But all writers need some time to clear their desks and their minds. While the body is otherwise occupied, the mind is preparing to write. It is almost as if, before you tackle the story, you have to prepare for the fight. You gird yourself mentally for what is to come.

4. Focusing Your Thoughts

Once you sit down to write, you need to sift through and evaluate all your material. This involves a careful rereading of all your notes, which by now should be waiting for you in readable form: sloppy handwritten notes and taped interviews should be typed up and clearly marked.

Plan to spend some time just going through all this information. Read it carefully. Underline different themes in your notes on the computer, or by hand on your paper with different colored pens.

Type an outline of your story, and leave lots of white

space to add marginal notes reminding you to add this quote here, that anecdote there. Tape a copy of the outline to your wall so you can see it. Modify it as needed. Each writer has her or his own way of focusing. Some make a duplicate set of all their notes, then cut one set into shreds and organize the shreds more or less the way the story will be organized. Some use index cards, putting one theme with all its subthemes on each card. You will have to try out different ways until you find the one that is most comfortable for you. The point is to have some sense of the *shape* of the story before you begin writing—or very soon thereafter. The shape may change, but begin with a plan just the same.

5. Writing

To maximize your productivity, make sure you have at least two hours of quiet and privacy. More is better, but most writers find they can't concentrate for more than three to four hours at a stretch. The telephone and visitors will destroy your work. Unplug the phone or turn on the answering machine (with the sound off, so you can't hear the messages). Don't plan to just let the phone ring: you will be constantly distracted wondering who's on the other end. Inform your friends, relatives, acquaintances, and all other people who might show up at your door that you will *not* answer the door during certain hours. You may have to post a note on the door, and leave paper and a pencil so visitors can leave you a note instead of buzzing.

Some people find it too distracting to work in their own house. If you do, then find another space in which to write: a small office, or the home of a friend who is away during your writing hours.

Allocate specific hours on specific days of the week for writing. Many writers like to plan to produce a certain number of pages during each writing session. If you set these kinds of goals, be sure they are reasonable and achievable. Every writer has his or her own speed, and some people write much faster than others. If you find your goals overly ambitious, adjust them. Otherwise you will end each writing day feeling you have failed, rather than feeling, as you should, that you have succeeded in that day's work. Keep in mind that even if you do decide to discard the results the next day, drafts that never make it past your circular file are still important stages to the final product.

When Norman Mailer was getting started as a writer, he would write four days a week: Mondays, Tuesdays, Thursdays, and Fridays. Each day, he would work from 10:00 A.M. to 12:30 P.M., then have lunch, then begin writing again at 2:30 or 3:00 P.M. for another two hours. He tried to average seven typewritten pages a day, twenty-eight pages a week.[3]

Ernest Hemingway, who used to write standing up, would mark on a chart the exact number of words he wrote each day. If he wanted to take the next day off to go fishing, he would write a little longer until he was satisfied with his word count.

The important thing is to write on a schedule. It should be part of your routine. Then, begin at the beginning. Try out some possible leads. If they don't work, save them, since you will probably be able to use some of them later in the body of the story. If you have trouble getting started, some writers suggest you "speedwrite" your way to a lead—just start typing, as quickly as possible, whatever you think the best lead might be. Don't aim for a perfect lead the first time around. You will refine, polish, and probably even change it as you move through your story. If writing a good lead seems to be intimidating, some suggest you begin writing in what you think is the middle of your story, and then work your way backwards to the lead. Also remember to write with a dictionary and a thesaurus nearby.

6. Editing

Try to let your story lie at least overnight, preferably a few days. Then begin to edit. Be as cruel as you can with yourself.

Before the story gets to a professional editor, many writers ask a relative, a friend, or a writer's group to read the story and evaluate it. Sometimes this can be helpful, even invaluable, if the person asked is good at editing. This kind of intervention has saved many a beginning writer from having a story rejected by an editor who didn't have the time or talent to fix it. But calling on a friend to edit also has its pitfalls: the friend may say it's great because he or she doesn't want to hurt your feelings, or doesn't know enough about writing to see what might be improved. If the friend can't write, he or she may be impressed by anyone who can write anything at all. So choose your "personal" editors with the same care you choose your "professional" editors. And if your spouse or mother says it's great, and your professional editor says it has lots of problems, be inclined to believe the second opinion.

But remember, of course, that from time to time professional editors have also been known to be wrong.

If you are lucky, you will have a *good* editor waiting for you at the newspaper, magazine, or publishing house for which you are writing. We have professional editors for our stories for the same reason we have professional teachers for our children: it is easier to discipline and train someone when you do not love them. Every writer needs a good editor; if you don't yet have one, look for one. Many writers write repeatedly for the same publication (even when they can get more money at others) because they value the talents of their editor.

These talents of an editor are different from those of a writer: good editors are not only whizzes at grammar and the basics of language, but they are also able to transform "prose [that] plods from one drab word to the next, all of them pedestrians"[4] into prose that strides with energy and purpose. They can spot the holes, the nonsequiturs, the flabby phrases, the disparities and unclarities, that even the best writer sometimes cannot see when the story in question is his or her own.

Above all, try to remove your ego from your story during the editing process. All writers, even the most experienced, tend to view their stories as little pieces of their own psyches, put out there on display for the world to appreciate. Remember that *you* are not your story. That when an editor is critiquing and criticizing your story, he or she is not attacking *you*. That when the editor says "this is confusing," or "that just doesn't work," he or she is not evaluating your IQ, your personality, even your talent; undoubtedly, he or she is not even *thinking* about your personality, your IQ, or your talent. An editor at work on a story has very narrow tunnel vision: the main concern is how to get the story in shape, how to make it work, how to adapt it to fit the publication. In short, the story is what is on the editor's mind, not you.

Editors are surprised when, in the middle of their attempts to articulate a problem in a story, the beginning writer suddenly bursts into tears (writers of both sexes have been known to do this); or when they happen to glance up and see that the writer's face has turned ghostly pale, or burning red. One editor, busily explaining the technical problems in a medical story to a writer, failed to notice the young man's increasing silence. Engrossed in the editing, the editor was amazed when the writer suddenly stood up, walked to the side of the editor's desk, and threw up into the wastebasket.

To an editor, a story is an object to be weighed and evaluated against other objects. To a writer, a story on which he or she has labored for days, weeks, or months is no longer an object, but is assimilated and absorbed until it is a subjective part of his or her being. The moral is: *Never take editing personally.* This takes a lot of practice, but after years of writing you may, in fact, achieve it.

7. Rewriting

A story is not finished once it is written. In fact, editing and rewriting are in some ways even more crucial. This does not mean you should write a story carelessly, as if it were a first draft. You should turn in a polished professional piece if you expect to be treated as a serious professional writer. But most stories need to have at least parts of them rewritten. The major writing problems that need to be tackled in a rewrite have been discussed in previous chapters: weak quotes, overwriting, clichés and other tired language, shaky organization, inadequate transitions, lack of color, vacillation in the writer's voice. Many stories need to be totally rewritten, and some need to be rewritten more than once. This holds true for experienced writers as well as novices. To minimize the amount of rewriting, it is best if you and the editor make absolutely sure you agree on the theme, tone, voice, and general substance of the article *before* you first write the story. If the theme, tone, voice, or substance changes as you gather information, tell the editor. Make an appointment if necessary, and discuss the changes in depth before you put a *word* on paper. Editors hate surprises. If they are expecting a story on types of marshmallows, don't turn in a story on ways of roasting them. Give them marshmallows, unless you have arranged ahead of time to focus on this new theme.

Remember this sage advice:

> If you're a supremely talented artist and you hit a very lucky day, then maybe you can write a poem or story or chapter or a novel that needs no revision. If you're a regular writer with your appointed portion of esthetic luck, you'll need to come at the piece again and again. I like to think of revision as a form of self-forgiveness: you can allow yourself mistakes and short-comings in your writing because you know you're coming back later to improve it. Revision is the way you cope with the bad luck that made your writing less than brilliant this morning.

Revision is the hope you hold out for yourself to make something beautiful tomorrow though you didn't quite manage
it today. Revision is democracy's literary method, the tool
that allows an ordinary person to aspire to extraordinary
achievement.[5]

❑ RESEARCH EXERCISES

Be patient; be self-forgiving; be willing to learn from your
own literary mistakes; and, above all, be brave enough to try
to write even better the next time around.

1. With a group of people, divide up the reference works
listed below and write a description that:

   A. tells how the reference is organized—for example, geo-
   graphically, chronologically, subject, title, author and
   so on;
   B. gives one example of a question that can be answered from
   the reference, with the answer and the page number where
   the answer can be found;
   C. indicates whether this information is available on a database and, if so, which one(s).

Acronyms, Initialisms and Abbreviations Dictionary
   Guide to more than 300,000 acronyms, initials, abbreviations, con-
   tractions, and alphabetic symbols.

Bartlett's Familiar Quotations
   Collection of passages, phrases, and proverbs traced to their sources
   in ancient and modern literature.

Black's Law Dictionary
   Description of legal terms, changes in legal concepts and doctrines.
   Describes federal acts, agencies, departments, and officials.

Congressional Information Service
   Brief abstracts of congressional publications containing information
   on committee hearings, House and Senate documents and reports,

and Senate treaty documents. Index of subjects, names (including witnesses at hearings), bill committee and subcommittee chairpersons, and so on.

Congressional Quarterly—Weekly
Reliable and extremely useful news service offering a weekly summary of congressional action and developments.

Congressional Quarterly—Annual
A survey of legislation for one session of Congress. Major congressional action is summarized. Includes voting information on individual measures.

County and City Data Book
The latest available census figures for each county and for large U.S. cities. Also includes summary figures for states, geographic regions, urban areas, and unincorporated places.

Editor and Publisher International Yearbook
A listing of all U.S. daily and weekly newspapers, with circulation rates, publishers and editors, syndicated services, schools of journalism, foreign correspondents, and daily newspapers in Canada and other countries.

Encyclopedia of Associations
A guide to about 18,000 national and international organizations, including trade, business, agriculture, government, public administration, legal, military, scientific, educational, cultural, social, welfare, religious, ethnic, hobby, and sports, as well as labor unions and chambers of commerce.

Europa Year Book
A guide to international organizations in Europe, Africa, the Americas, Asia, and Australasia. For each country, it has an introductory survey, a statistical survey, and information on politics, religion, the print and broadcast media, trade and industry, tourism, atomic energy, and so on.

Facts on File
Weekly classified digest of news arranged under such headings as World Affairs, National Affairs, Latin America, Finance, Economy, Arts, Science, and so forth. Published twice a month. The annual bound volume is called *Facts on File Yearbook.*

Famous First Facts
A record of more than 9,000 first happenings, discoveries, and inventions in American history.

Gallup Polls
Presents all the statistical data from more than 7,000 polls of American political and social opinion.

Guinness Book of World Records
Compendium of information concerning the longest, shortest, tallest, deepest, fastest, and other superlatives pertaining to natural and manmade phenomena and human events and achievements.

Hammond World Atlases
Includes maps of the world, postal zip codes for the United States, historical maps, section called "Environment and Life," population figures, reproductions of flags, and small topographical maps.

Information Please Almanac, Atlas, and Yearbook
An almanac of miscellaneous information, including extensive statistical and historical information on the United States; chronology of the year's events; statistical and historical descriptions of other countries; sports records; motion picture, theatrical, and literary awards; celebrated persons; and so on.

Moody's Industrial Manual
Extensive information on New York, regional, and national companies listed on the stock exchanges.

The New Encyclopaedia Britannica
The most famous encyclopedia in English. The 10-volume Micropaedia offers brief factual information on 102,000 subjects. The 19-volume Macropaedia has 4,200 detailed, longer articles on many subjects.

Rand-McNally Commercial Atlas and Marketing Guide
Primarily an atlas of America, but includes a section with maps of foreign countries. Also has statistical tables of population, business and manufacturing, agriculture, and so forth.

Security Dealers of North America
Up-to-date listing of stock and bond dealers in the United States and Canada.

Standard and Poors—Ratings Guide
Lists corporate bonds, commercial paper, municipal bonds, and international securities. Explains what ratings are, and how they are used.

Standard and Poors—Stock Market Encyclopedia
Includes two pages of information on each stock on all American stock exchanges.

Statesman's Yearbook
> Concise descriptive and statistical information about the governments of the world.

Statistical Abstract of the United States
> Published by the Bureau of the Census. Summary statistics on the political, social, and economic complexion of the United States.

Ulrich's International Periodicals Directory
> Classified list of about 65,000 periodicals from around the world. "One of the ten source books a librarian would take to a desert island," claims my local librarian.

U.S. Government Manual
> The official organization handbook of the federal government, with information on the activities and officials of the various departments, bureaus, offices, and so on. Includes charts of more complex agencies.

Webster's Biographical Dictionary
> Dictionary of noteworthy persons, living and deceased, with pronunciations and concise biographies.

Who's Who
> More than 120 books, listing prominent persons in many professions and nations.

World Almanac and Book of Facts
> Most comprehensive American almanac of miscellaneous information. Includes statistics on social, industrial, political, financial, religious, educational, and other subjects.

2. Do the same as in exercise 1 for the following reference works—and also provide your own succinct description of each work. Again, it is more fun to divide this exercise among several people, and then share what you have learned.

Celebrity Register
Contemporary Authors

The New York Times Index
The Los Angeles Times Index

Who's Who in Finance and Industry
Who's Who in the West

Books in Print
The Reader's Guide to Periodical Literature

Official Congressional Directory
A Citizen's Guide to Congress

Sylvia Porter's New Money Book for the 80's
Moody's Handbook of Common Stocks
Index of Corporations and Industries

Humanities Index
Social Sciences Index

Vital Speeches of the Day
Simpson's Contemporary Quotations

Current Biography
Who Was Who

Famous First Facts
Facts on File

The World Almanac
Columbia Lippincott Gazetteer of the World

Yearbook of the United Nations
United Nations Statistical Yearbook

□ 9 □

SELLING IT

FOR THOSE WHO SELL their work free-lance—or who plan to do so in the near future—here are some tips.

There are two ways to market a story: you can write it on speculation (called "on spec"), or write it on assignment. To write *on spec* means you have an idea, and an editor somewhere likes the idea and promises to look at your finished manuscript to see if he or she might be willing to publish it. The editor has no *obligation* to publish it. The writer takes all the chances.

To write *on assignment* means you have an idea, you query an editor about it—either in an informal conversation, or in a formal written proposal—and the editor agrees to publish the story. This means that, barring unforeseen hitches, the editor has a commitment—perhaps legal, at least ethical—to publish it. The writer's risk is reduced.

Almost all beginning free-lance writers are asked to write on spec at least once, and sometimes a few times, until an editor knows and trusts his or her work. Then an editor may make a firm assignment, which should be backed up with a written confirmation of the terms of the assignment (see chapter 10, "Your Rights and Responsibilities").

Even for those who want to be magazine writers, writing for newspapers is often a good way to begin to get clips, which will help you get assignments later from other, perhaps bigger, newspapers, and from magazines. Newspaper editors are often easier to reach; they may also be publishing features on a daily or weekly basis and are hungry for fresh ideas and good writers. As a result, newspaper editors are more likely to give you a chance—even to give you an assignment based on an informal telephone conversation. Since newspapers run shorter features (except for the magazine sections), it is usually less of an investment to research and write the story even on spec. Be forewarned, however, that smaller community papers may not pay you anything (and even the largest newspapers have relatively small free-lance budgets and don't pay much). You may get only $200 for a 1,500-word feature in a large circulation newspaper, whereas you can get $1,500 for a comparable feature in a national magazine. But most writers start out small (both in terms of circulation and income for their stories) and work their way up. The important thing in the beginning is to accumulate a clip file and a track record of productive working relationships with professional editors.

The following scenario will give you an idea of how to proceed as you try and sell your story.

Finding the Right Market

Once you have an idea for a story, you have to find the right place to publish it. It is crucial to *tailor the story* for the publication. *Texas Monthly* is not interested in a story on your vacation in Kashmir, India, unless it has a unique and compelling Texas angle; your local Texas paper might be, however, since the story is about the experiences of a local resident. *Redbook* is not interested in a story on depression in elderly men (their market is younger, married women); *Psychology Today* might be, however. Become familiar with the publications for which you want to write: read them on a regular basis. Nothing will kill your publication chances faster than to propose an idea and be told by the editor: if you read us, you would know we (a) did that story six months ago, or (b) never do that kind of story.

Several good reference books will help you match your ideas with a market. Many beginning free-lancers buy at least one of them to keep at home, but you can also find them at your local library. They include:

Writer's Market: Where & How To Sell What You Write: This lists more than 4,000 magazines, newsletters, and syndicates to which to sell your free-lance writing. The introduction contains pragmatic advice on selling and reselling your articles, copyright law, and sample query letters.

Gale Directory of Publications: This gives detailed information about all daily and weekly newspapers and periodicals in the United States and Canada, including phone numbers, addresses, names of all editors. Especially valuable is a separate list of the names of all feature editors of the most popular features sections appearing in daily newspapers with a circulation of 50,000 or more.

Editor and Publisher International Yearbook: This lists every daily and weekly newspaper and syndicate in the United States and the world, including foreign-language papers. It gives addresses, circulation, telephone numbers, and names of editors.

You can also pick the editor's name off the masthead. But the above books grow quickly out-of-date, and even a current issue of a magazine may have been printed two months earlier. Whatever your source, always *call* the publication you have in mind, and double-check (with either the switchboard operator or the editor's secretary or assistant) the name and title of the editor with whom you plan to communicate. The call will probably take less than three minutes, and it is worth the message units. Editors tend to change jobs frequently, and the information you have may be outdated. Editors find it annoying if you write or call the wrong person to make your pitch. It shows you have not done your research at even this early stage. As a result, some won't even want to deal with you.

Contacting the Editor

Once you've targeted one or several markets, the next step is to decide on a plan of attack: should you call the editor, or should you write first? For newspapers, and for small- to medium-sized magazines, the most expeditious strategy is to call first, and see how far you get. It is surprising how often you may be able to speak to the editor about your idea, and how many editors are willing to return your phone calls if you leave a message and a brief synopsis of why you are calling. Before you call, outline either in your mind or on paper how you plan to present your idea, so you are not caught off guard. Sound professional. You will be nervous, but editors usually understand that, and may even sympathize.

The important thing is to be succinct. Editors, like writers, are usually underpaid and overworked. Don't waste their time. Sound enthusiastic, self-confident, and competent. Listen carefully to what they have to say, then get off the line.

If you are unsure which editor among the array listed on the masthead is the best one for you to contact, then start with the top editor (not the publisher) and work your way down. The editor-in-chief or managing editor will probably *not* be the person who deals directly with free-lance writers, but his or her secretary can tell you who does. Occasionally, you may even get the top editor on the line, who will hear you out and advise you on how to proceed. If you start at the top, you have the added advantage of then using that editor's name when you place your next call or send your letter to a subordinate editor: "Editor So-and-So's office told me to get in touch with you . . ." if you've spoken to the secretary; or, better yet, "Editor So-and-So told me to get in touch with you . . ." if you've spoken with the editor him/herself.

Many editors will cringe when they read the above ad-vice, because they don't want to be swamped with calls from eager but inexperienced writers. In fact, if an editor is asked whether a writer should call or write with a story idea, the editor almost 100 percent of the time says "write." A letter is more convenient for the editor, who can then consider your written proposal in due course, and respond when it best suits him or her. A letter will also show the editor how succinctly you can write. From the editor's point of view, written com-munication is preferable.

From the writer's point of view, however, it is prob-lematic for several reasons.

First, it is always better to have voice contact with some-one in the publication. Not only editors, but also secretaries can be powerful allies. If you receive your information from a secretary, be sure to write down the secretary's name and title (it may be "editorial assistant" or some variation), and convey a gracious thank-you before getting off the line.

Second, by calling you are being assertive rather than passive; you are doing what many writers dare not do, because they feel too intimidated. You have set yourself apart from the crowd. You may not get too far. You may be told: "We don't consider any assignments over the phone. You'll have to send a query letter," in which case go ahead and send the letter, mentioning, however, that you did call and you understand from So-and-So this is the way to proceed. This also helps if you don't get an answer by mail, and you need to make one or several follow-up calls. For when you call, you may then say: "I wrote at the suggestion of So-and-So, and since I have not received a response I am calling back to find out the status of my proposal."

Third, when you call you may well receive from the editor a quick answer to the question of whether or not the publication would consider your article. If the feedback is negative ("That story doesn't sound right for us") you may be able to explore a new angle or another story idea that fits better. If not, you have saved yourself at least two weeks of waiting for the negative answer in the mail. You can skip that publication and go on to the next one.

Writing a Query Letter When Called For

The writing of query letters is an art in itself. The query letter is, basically, a press release for your story: it has to *sell* the story to your editor. Your own query should do the following:

Be Brief.   Editors often say they like to see one-page queries, and that is sufficient for many articles. However, since much of the first page is taken up with the formalities of the heading, one-and-a-half pages is all right for queries on longer stories.

You can count on the editor not reading past the second page. As an editor from the *New York Times Magazine* once explained: "Great minds have short attention spans." Another reason is the stack of other queries and unsolicited manuscripts piled nearby, waiting for their attention.

Be Polished.   The query must be addressed to the right person, with the correct title and address. The person's name *must be spelled correctly without any variations whatsoever.* Don't assume Ann Marie's name has no *e* on the end of Ann, and no hyphen between Ann and Marie. Don't assume Murphy is spelled with a "phy"; it might be spelled Murfee. Check. The query must, of course, be typed. It must be letter perfect and contain no typos. Otherwise, chances are great it will be placed in the circular file below the editor's desk.

Be Snappy.   Hook the editor into the query with a strong lead. Use a few statistics, and perhaps an anecdote, to show you have done basic research. Be succinct.

Outline Your Approach. Tell the editor in the query *exactly* what you plan to cover in the story, and how you plan to do it. Be as specific as possible, so there is no room for future misunderstanding about the scope or tone of the story.

Be Appropriate. Write the query in the style of the publication to which you are submitting it. Be erudite for *Harper's,* short and snappy for *Parade.* Make it clear you know the audience of that particular publication. Don't propose a local story for a national publication, unless you can show why it is of national interest. Don't propose a national story for a local publication, unless you have a local angle.

Be Self-confident. Avoid "wounded elk" query letters that begin: "I don't know if you'll be interested in this, but . . ." or "I've never published before, but . . ." Sell your competence in your query.

Give Your Credentials. In a brief paragraph at the *end,* tell the editor where you have been published, and attach a few clips (only a few!) if you think it will help. If you have not published, and have no clips, give whatever credentials you have that will make you credible. Explain why you have special knowledge, insight, or interest in this story. Do not, under any circumstances, apologize for yourself ("I've only published in my hometown paper, but I'm sure I can do the job . . . .").

Omit Business Details. Do not bring up issues of payment, copyright, expenses, deadline, or any of the other nitty-gritty details. They will come up later if the editor is interested (see chapter 10, "Your Rights and Responsibilities").

End Gracefully. Tell the editor that you look forward to speaking with him or her about the story. Include your name, mailing address, and telephone numbers.

After you have mailed in your query, give the editor at least two weeks to respond. If you haven't heard anything by the third week, a brief, polite phone call may be enough to jog an answer. The longer the wait, the less likely it is they were taken by the idea. However, responses also get delayed by vacations, illness, a change of staff or owners. Sometimes the assigning editor will love the idea, kick it upstairs, and wait for weeks for an answer to filter back down. A writer may sit on tenterhooks for a couple of months, then call only to learn that the editor's mail has been unopened for weeks, or your query has been lost, or the editor is waiting for an answer from another editor. A quick phone call can alleviate a lot of double guessing.

If repeated phone calls (say, one a week after the first two weeks have passed) bring no positive response, then just quietly give up, and send the query on to the next publication. The worst that can happen is that two publications will want to buy your story. The odds are greatly against this, however.

A few writers send out multiple queries on the same idea, but most editors feel this is an unfair practice. Each editor likes to have the unique right to review your proposal, and reject or accept your story. It is obviously to the writer's advantage to send out multiple queries, however, since it saves a lot of time waiting for a linear series of rejections.

And the fact is that most story ideas *are* rejected, which is why some people who are trying to make a living by free-lance writing send out three or more queries to different publications on different topics at one time.

The industry rule, however, is that you are supposed to "confess" if you are committing the crime of sending out multiple queries. If you confess, it means that you may harm your chances by telling the editor that you are also querying others. On the other hand, if you don't tell the editor, then you are considered guilty of hiding something—a professional breach of faith. Editors, of course, do not face similar constraints. They have the right to consider several queries on similar or related topics, choose one writer to handle the story, and then give that writer "advice" for the approach based in part on the other queries that were rejected. This is one of the inequities faced by free-lance feature writers. You have to decide for yourself which route you want to take.

Beginning writers sometimes worry that if they send in a query their idea will be stolen outright and given to another writer. While an editor may "spin off" a query, and consciously or subconsciously pass information along to another writer who may be working on the same topic, it is rare— surprisingly rare, in fact—for publications to outright steal ideas. When it does happen, it may result in a lawsuit, with the publication paying damages to a writer who can prove the idea was stolen. The problem is that so few ideas are unique: chances are your wonderful idea is someone else's wonderful idea as well. When topics become "hot"—for women's magazines battered women, working mothers, and single parents come to mind—editors are not only flooded with queries related to them, but are also making their own assignments on these topics to writers whose work they know.

Your challenge—as new writer on the block—is to write such a compelling query that it outshines the others. If an editor is impressed with the writing in your query but not with the particular idea, the editor will usually encourage you to submit other ideas, and you should do so, until you finally get an assignment.

▫ **10** ▫

YOUR RIGHTS AND RESPON-SIBILITIES

EVERY TIME YOU SELL an article free-lance to a publication, you have entered into a unique business agreement. It may be in the form of a legal contract, or a letter from the editor to you, or from you to the editor (called a "letter of agreement"). In some cases—with smaller newspapers or magazines—the agreement may be verbal. It is a good idea, however, to take notes during the conversation and send the editor a note confirming the details, with a copy for your file, in case of future misunderstanding about the terms of the story.

Negotiating the Business Details

After you are assigned a story, iron out the business details right away. The items to be covered, preferably in writing include:

1. The General Subject of the Story.   This includes any special angle or treatment.

2. The Deadline.   This will range from a week or two for a brief, newspaper-length feature, to a few months for a longer magazine piece. Be sure to set a realistic deadline that you know you can meet.

3. The Number of Words.   Try to produce an article that is as close as possible to the number of words agreed upon. Editors despair when pieces come in far too long; it usually means a major rewrite and lots of heavy editing. They are also suspicious if it comes in far too short, for it may reflect inadequate research. If you see your article is running long, alert the editor ahead of time.

4. Payment.   This includes the amount of money to be paid, and how soon after acceptance of the manuscript payment will be made. Publications are dragging their corporate heels more and more when it comes to paying their writers. This is usually not the fault of the editor, but is a policy (usually informal) of the parent company, which wants to hang on to its money as long as possible. Payment should be made within two weeks (ten working days) after acceptance. It should *not* be made on *publication.* Too many writers who wait to be paid on publication never see their money. If the publication folds, or is sold, or a new editor comes in and decides to clear the old inventory and make a fresh start, the writer is the first to suffer.

5. Kill Fee.   This is the amount of money the publication agrees to give you if the editors consider the manuscript unsuitable, even after a rewrite. It usually runs one-third to one-fourth of the agreed upon full fee. (More on the kill fee in a moment.)

6. Expenses. Put in writing what expenses the publication will cover (telephone, travel, research costs) and up to how much it will pay. Save your receipts, keep an itemized diary of costs, and you will be reimbursed after you have turned in the story. In some cases, publications will provide some expense money up front, especially if it involves travel—airline tickets, hotels, or car rentals. Agreed-upon expenses should be paid even if the publication does not use ("kills") your story.

7. Feedback. After receiving the manuscript, the decision on acceptance or rejection should be made fairly quickly. Most writer's organizations agree that four weeks is the absolute limit to allow for this; most editors can give you a decision in one to two weeks.

8. Copyright. You should agree to give the publication first North American serial rights *only.* (More on this in a minute.)

9. Editing. The editor should consult with you before making any substantive changes in your copy. This includes adding, deleting, or moving around material in the feature. You have the right to see galleys of your story in time to approve changes made by the editors.

Here is a standard format for your letter of agreement:[1]

Editor's Name
Editor's Title
Publication
Address

Dear Editor's Name:

This will confirm our agreement that I have been assigned to write an article of [NUMBER] words for [NAME OF PUBLICATION] on the subject of [BRIEF DESCRIPTION], per our conversation of [DATE].

The deadline for delivery of this article to you is [DATE].

My fee for this article is [DOLLAR AMOUNT], payable within two weeks after acceptance of the manuscript. You will notify me within two weeks after receipt of the manuscript whether it has been accepted.

[NAME OF PUBLICATION] shall be entitled to first North American serial rights.

If the completed manuscript is unacceptable to the editors even after revisions, a kill fee of [DOLLAR AMOUNT] shall be paid. If the completed manuscript is not accepted or not published through no fault of the author, then the full fee shall be paid.

It is understood that you shall reimburse me for up to [DOLLAR AMOUNT] of expenses incurred in the research and writing of the article, include telephone calls, Xeroxing, and [SPECIFY ALL ITEMS]. Should additional expenses be necessary, it is agreed that I will discuss them with you before they are incurred.

It is also agreed that you will submit galleys of the article for my examination far enough ahead of publication for me to review the final version, and correct errors.

Sincerely,

Name
Address
Phone
Social Security Number

Managing Common Problems

While the above nine points seem straightforward enough, they are fraught with peril. Almost anything can—and has—

gone wrong with these agreements, usually to the writer's detriment.

Let's consider the following not atypical scenarios.

SCENARIO 1:

You have an assignment. You are pleased. You do the story, turn it in on deadline, and you wait. And wait. And wait. Has the story been accepted? Rejected? Does it need a rewrite? Repeated calls to the editor do not produce satisfactory results. One month passes, then two. Soon the story will be too old to use. It will need to be updated. What should you do?

First, every publication has its own process for making editorial decisions. Usually, more than one editor needs to review the manuscript and suggest changes. After everyone has his or her say, you will finally receive an answer. Let's say the answer is: "It has promise, but we'd like you to take another stab at it." In other words, the editors want a rewrite. Your editor sends you a typed, carefully outlined list of all the proposed changes. So you re-interview, do new interviews, shift the focus, change the structure, and resubmit.

SCENARIO 2:

From here, several things can happen. First, the rewrite can be fine. Second, the editors want other changes made, or want parts of the original story re-incorporated. Often, the editors are right—the revisions do improve the piece. Sometimes, however, editors are inexperienced, or uncertain, or in disagreement among themselves about whether and how the story could be improved.

Every experienced writer has suffered at least once from editorial ambivalence. The editors of a national women's magazine, for instance, told a highly experienced writer (more than one hundred articles in major magazines) to rewrite an assigned article so that the information near the end was brought up to the top, and the information near the top was dropped down to the end. This involved a major overhaul of the entire structure of the story. It took the writer days to rewrite. She turned it in, and then received an apologetic phone call: the editors decided they liked the first version better after all.

Scenario 3:

The third scenario is that the editors decide your story is beyond repair, and tell you they are killing the story. If, in fact, you have not really done your job well, then it is best to take the kill fee without complaint. However, stories are often killed through no fault of the writer. If this is the case, you should insist upon receiving the full fee. The most common no-fault circumstances include:

- your editor left, and the new editor wants to use his/her own writers
- the owner left, and the new owner is aiming for a slightly different market
- the editors couldn't make a timely decision on the story, and now it is too old to use
- the editors like the story, but a superior will not run it for political reasons
- the editors like the story, but they hadn't realized someone else was working on a similar piece
- the editors like the story but feel—for some vague reason—it is just "not right" for them (this is usually a camouflage for one of the above)

Keep in mind that editors, who like to nurture their good writers, often feel equally frustrated by these events, which are frequently beyond their control.

Other possible disasters may befall your manuscript. For

instance, it has happened that a magazine accepts an article, pays for it, and then never publishes it. Month after month, the writer calls. It is scheduled, rescheduled. The editors love it but no one else will ever get a chance to read it.

When this happens, try telling the magazine you will be delighted if and when it is printed, but meanwhile you are going to try and resell it elsewhere before it gets too stale. This often breaks the logjam: it gives your editor, who may feel just as annoyed by the situation as you do, ammunition to aim up the line, so he or she can apply the needed pressure to spring your story from its limbo.

In the book publishing industry, authors have successfully fought in court to keep book advances they received from publishers who accepted their manuscript for publication, but then failed to distribute the book once it was printed—in effect, killing the book. Similarly, organizations representing free-lance writers feel that if a magazine does not publish your accepted article within a reasonable amount of time, the writer may reclaim and resell it without returning any payment. But "a reasonable amount of time" is a vague indicator: the American Society of Journalists and Authors (ASJA) believes that "if after six months the publisher has not scheduled an article for publication, or within twelve months has not published an article," the manuscript and all rights should revert to the author.

Some features obviously have to be moved into print faster than that. You will have to negotiate each situation as it arises, but in general any story held longer than three months is getting dangerously stale. Most major publications understand this, and will pay you to update your story if they hold it too long.

If you want to resell your story, discuss your options with your original editor. You may be advised to return to magazine #1 the payment you received from it (or whatever portion thereof you receive from magazine #2). Or you may be told you can simply accept payment from magazine #2 and not

repay magazine #1. Some magazines, under these circumstances, don't expect repayment. Some do. One writer made
$4,000 by reselling an article several times before it was finally
published.

SCENARIO 4:

A fourth scenario is that your article, once it appears in print,
has been edited beyond recognition. One national women's
magazine is notorious among writers for making up quotes
and descriptions to "jazz up" a story. While many editors
faithfully report to writers any changes made in their copy,
some editors are not so diligent. The PEN Standards for Magazine and Periodical Assignments also warns that the editor
should

> not do violence to the intent and spirit of an article through
> the use of headlines, cover lines, subheads, break heads, illus-
> trations, captions, identification boxes, and the like; that writ-
> ers make known to the editor their feelings, and request
> consultation, about any of these production procedures; and
> that editors recognize an obligation to respond to these feel-
> ings insofar as the mechanics of production permit.

Because of the many hitches that may appear in the editing process, it is important to see galleys well before the story
hits the newsstands. If changes have been made that you cannot live with and that your editor refuses to correct, you can
at least insist that your byline be removed from the story.

When Melissa Ludtke Lincoln wrote a profile of Reggie
Jackson for a national woman's magazine, she recalled that in
the editing

> quotes were reworded in ways that changed their meaning.
> Descriptions of Jackson's mood during the interview were
> manufactured. For example, one editor wrote in, "Reggie is

getting angry. Though his voice is steady, his eyes are cold as dry ice." In fact, Reggie was at that moment completely dispassionate. That and a number of other changes in the tone, angle and accuracy of the article were all termed "trivial" by the editor, who told me I had a lot to learn about journalism if I thought that a writer had the right to rework an editor's version. After close to six months of work on that article, I insisted that it be published . . . under a fake by-line. That proved to be my only comeback.[2]

Protecting Your Copyright

If you are writing on assignment for a publication owned by a large company—such as Condé Nast or Hearst—you will be sent a contract to sign and return, rather than a more informal letter of agreement. The contract will contain the information outlined in the above letter of agreement, and if it has omitted any of the details, add them to the contract, or outline them in a separate attached letter when returning the contract. If you add to or change anything on the contract, be sure to initial those places.

Many of these legal contracts contain two clauses that writers should watch out for. One involves copyright. The old copyright law, dating from 1909, required an author to publish the work, with the correct notice of copyright, in order to obtain copyright protection. You no longer need to do this. The new Copyright Act that took effect in 1978 protects all authors by automatically granting them copyright upon the creation of their own work. "When the author types the manuscript of his or her novel, poem, play, or article or writes it in longhand or dictates it into a recording machine, then the work is copyrighted," says Irwin Karp, an attorney specializing in copyright issues.

Now, *you* hold the exclusive rights to reproduce and distribute your article, and lose those rights only by signing them away in a contract, or by agreeing passively to a letter of assignment which takes them away. If you receive a contract that takes away anything other than first North American serial rights, you can cross out all the other variations and initial the changes before returning the signed contract.

In a survey of twenty-four publications that handle free-lance work, each one asked its writers to give up some portion of their copyright.[3]

"It's an increasingly bad situation," says Donald Robinson, chair of the contracts committee of ASJA. "And because assignments are becoming more difficult to get, writers will sign anything. It is clear that a climate has been created that fosters violations in spirit—if not in law—of the Copyright Act."

The two most prevalent forms of trying to defeat the basic aim of the new copyright law are the "grab-all" contract, in which the writer is intimidated into letting the magazine take all rights for itself, and the 50 percent clause, which, in effect, makes the magazine a private syndicate by allowing it to keep half of future reprint profits from an article. "I tell our members both these terms are unacceptable," says Murray Bloom, who has been handling editor-writer relations for ASJA for 29 years.

Free-lancers often agree to give up their rights to control the artistic use of, and receive financial gain from, their work not only out of eagerness to publish, but also out of ignorance. "Basically, writers are not too astute about contracts," says an editor at a men's magazine, who asked to remain anonymous. "The editor can send out whatever he thinks the writer will sign."

It is understandable that magazines need to protect their own interests to ensure that they will be first to publish an article in their circulation area, even to ensure that they won't be sued for copyright infringement if the magazine is sold in a foreign PX. But magazines that now ask for "all rights" or "world periodical rights" or "all rights North American" or "first-time world rights" are playing variations on the theme of copyright erosion. Some publications even insist that freelancers sign a "work-for-hire" agreement, which takes advantage of a loophole in the copyright law that allows the publisher to treat the writer as an employee whose work belongs to the corporation once it is created. If you sign a work-for-hire agreement, you sign away your copyright.

It is easy to blame editors for this copyright tug-of-war, since they are the ones with whom writers negotiate. But editors are often not the enemy. "Editors often have the writer's point of view, and are extremely uncomfortable about the contracts they're asked to send out," says ASJA's Robinson. "But their individual judgment and ability to act have been severely curtailed and guided by the overall policy of the front office."

In fact, top management at some magazines tells its editors to offer from two to five different contracts, each one with separate copyright terms, depending on what the author is willing to settle for and how badly the editor wants the article.

The best each free-lancer can hope for is to insist on retaining as much of his or her copyright as possible at the moment when the terms of an assignment are being negotiated. Under certain circumstances, simply crossing out and initialing offensive parts of a contract may protect a writer from its terms, says Stanley Rothenberg, a New York copyright attorney.

The second nefarious clause appearing in more freelance contracts is the blanket indemnification clause. These are often written in hazy legalese, but at their worst they mean the author must pay all legal expenses to defend any lawsuit arising over his or her article, no matter how ludicrous the charge. A typical contract reads:

> The author agrees to indemnify and hold harmless [THIS MAGAZINE] against any loss, damage or expense (including

attorney's fees) or recovery arising from or related to any breach or alleged breach of the warranties. If any claim, demand, action or proceeding is successfully defended, however, the author's indemnity shall be limited to 50 percent of such costs and expenses.

This means if someone sues the magazine over something you wrote, you pay all the costs if you lose, half the costs if you win.

Some free-lancers routinely cross out indemnity clauses along with copyright infringement clauses. Lawyers agree that this alteration will protect your copyright, but disagree on whether it in any way limits liability. While writers' groups disapprove of indemnity clauses, they seem to have little power to do anything about them right now. The National Writers' Union's Code of Minimum Practice, for instance, says that

in the case of a libel action, the writer shall support the publisher by appearing in defense if so requested. The publisher shall provide like support for the writer. In either case, the publisher shall provide legal counsel and assume moral and financial responsibility unless the writer is found to be at fault.

That is the theory, but no longer the practice. It will probably take several court cases to establish some new ground rules in this area.

On the next page is a sample magazine contract, marked with appropriate deletions.

SAMPLE MAGAZINE CONTRACT*

TO: AUTHOR   DATE:
    ADDRESS
This will confirm the agreement between us with respect to the
literary material entitled [WORKING TITLE OF ARTICLE] by
[NAME OF AUTHOR] submitted by [NAME OF AUTHOR
OR AGENT] as follows:

1. The Author hereby grants to [NAME OF CORPORATE
OWNER] and to its licensees, first North American serial rights
only; ~~and assigns to them forever, all rights in and to the Material
and all rights of copyright therein, including, but without limita-
tion, the exclusive right to publish the Material in magazine,
newspaper and book form, and to use it in dramatic, motion
picture, radio and television productions anywhere. The rights
herein granted include the right to: edit, revise, abridge, condense and translate the Material; to publish the same in one or
more installments; to change the title thereof;~~ to use the Author's
name, biography and likeness in connection with the publication, advertising and promotion of the Material; and to make
such other promotional use of the material as [THE PUBLICA-
TION], its licensees or assignees may determine.

2. In full payment for the rights herein granted by the Author,
[NAME OF PUBLICATION] agrees to pay to the Author or
the Agent the sum of [$ AMOUNT] within fifteen days after the
execution and delivery of this Agreement.*

3. The Author warrants: that the Author to the best of her
knowledge is the author and sole owner of the Material; that it
is original and has never been published in any form; that it
contains no matter unlawful in content or violative of the rights
of any third party; that the rights granted hereunder are free and
clear; and that the author has full power to grant such rights. ~~The
Author agrees to hold [THE PUBLICATION] harmless from
any claims arising out of the breach of this paragraph.~~

> Please acknowledge your agreement to the foregoing by signing and returning one copy of this letter.
>
> The Editor

*In some cases, the author is not mailed this contract until *after* the article has been completed and accepted by the publication. This contract—and its timing—usually comes as an unpleasant surprise to an author the first time it happens. By sending a contract after the article is completed, the corporation adds pressure on the author to sign the contract as is, since she or he has already invested the time in writing the article.

Your Allies

Who are your allies in free-lance writing?

1. First, *your editor,* who is usually sympathetic to the problems of his or her writers.
2. Next, *the fact-checker.* Most large magazines now use fact-checkers, who will call you soon after your story is accepted and tell you they plan to check your sources. Some ask you to turn over your files. Writers may bristle at the thought that someone is checking up on them, but good fact-checkers have saved many writers from embarrassment. It is helpful, when you finish a story, to draw up a list for the fact-checker of the names and telephone numbers of all your sources in the story. If you have confidential sources, you will have to talk with your editor about how to handle them. Some writers turn over the names and numbers of people quoted anonymously in articles, with an alert to the fact-checker to reassure these sources that they will remain anonymous even though quotes and informa-

tion from them are being verified. Other writers refuse to do this.

Newspapers, however, do not use fact-checkers, and it is inadvisable under any circumstances to depend on a fact-checker to catch an error of fact, or help out with free research assistance. You alone are ultimately responsible for the accuracy of every fact in your story.

You are also responsible for making sure that every word in your story belongs to you and has not been plagiarized—inadvertently or intentionally—from another writer's work. *Plagiarism* means to use another writer's words or ideas without giving that writer credit. This literary theft can run the gamut from outright wholesale copying, to paraphrasing another writer without attribution, to lifting a quote that first appeared in someone else's story. Many a promising writing career has been ruined by plagiarism.

3. An *agent* can be useful in handling some of the problems listed in this chapter. But most writers—even those with agents for their books—do not use agents for magazine work. And most agents are not interested in magazine work, because there is so little money in it for them. Agents who do handle magazine work take 10 to 15 percent of the fee you receive.

Several writers' organizations can also provide useful clout.

4. Among the largest dealing with authors' rights is *The American Society of Journalists and Authors.* ASJA represents approximately 750 free-lance writer members, and is active in protecting their rights. It publishes a confidential newsletter on the free-lance business that includes members' experiences—good and bad—with dozens of magazines. It also publishes a very useful guide, *The ASJA Handbook: A Writer's Guide to Ethical and Economic Issues,* which you may get by sending $5.95 to: ASJA, 1501 Broadway, Room 1907, New York, NY 10036. To become a member, you must in the past two to four years have published eight articles or one book, with a second under contract. Interested writers can call the ASJA offices: (212) 997-0947.

5. *The National Writers' Union.* This feisty and growing union has about 2,500 members in twelve local chapters around the country. It helps resolve disputes between free-lancers and book or magazine publishers, and publishes a newsletter with tips for writers. The union has also negotiated contracts with eight magazines and newspapers governing the standards of treatment for free-lancers. Membership is open to virtually everyone: you need only show that you are attempting to publish your writing. Interested writers are encouraged to call the national headquarters: (212) 254-0279. The address is: National Writers' Union, 13 Astor Place, 7th Floor, New York, NY 10003.

6. *PEN American Center.* This is an international association of book authors, and it also publishes brochures on authors' and translators' rights. These are available by writing to: PEN American Center, 568 Broadway, 4th Floor, New York, NY 10012. PEN is especially active in freedom-of-the-press issues in the United States and abroad. Membership requirements include two published books of "literary merit." For information on PEN's programs, call (212) 334-1660.

7. *The Authors Guild.* This group, too, focuses on book authors, but its newsletter provides useful information on the publishing industry. It is especially strong in the legal aspects of publishing, and has represented authors in a number of landmark cases. It also lobbies in Washington on copyright and tax legislation issues. To become a member, you must have published one book by an established American publisher in the last seven years, or three magazine articles in regularly circulating magazines in the last eighteen months. Those with a book contract pending may join as an associate member. Its address is: The Authors Guild, 234 West 44th Street, New York, NY 10036. For membership information, call (212) 398-0838.

APPENDIX:
Read Well to
Write Well

HERE IS A list of suggested readings. Add to it. If you start a book that does not appeal to you, put it away for another day. To love a book, you must come to it at the right time in your life.

While reading, ask yourself the following questions:

- What point of view does the writer adopt toward the subject? How is that view manifested in the writing?
- Does the writer have an ear for dialogue? How does she or he handle quotes?
- How often does the writer use description? Anecdote?
- How does the writer handle statistics?
- Do you hear the writer's voice? What kind of voice is it?
- How does the writer convey his or her opinions?
- How has the writer structured the book? (Outline a chapter or even the entire book.)
- Is the writing difficult or easy for you to read? Why?
- Is it boring or interesting? Why?

- What is your favorite part of the book? Why?
- What annoys you?
- What would you like to imitate from this writer's style?

GREAT NONFICTION

Baldwin, James, *The Fire Next Time*. New York: Dell, 1985. (A personal and historical account about the reality of being black in America)

Best Newspaper Writing, edited by Don Fry. St. Petersburg, Florida: The Poynter Institute for Media Studies. (Annual collection of stories since 1979 that won awards from the American Society of Newspaper Editors)

Capote, Truman, *In Cold Blood*. New York: Signet, 1965. (Early, powerful "new journalism": the nonfiction novel)

Didion, Joan, *Slouching Towards Bethlehem*. New York: Washington Square Press/Simon & Schuster, 1983. (Reporting on the sixties)

Dillard, Annie, *Pilgrim at Tinker Creek*. New York: Bantam, 1974. (A mystical excursion into the world of nature)

Fallaci, Oriana, *Interview With History*. Boston: Houghton Mifflin, 1977. (Aggressive interviewing of the famous)

Fitzgerald, Frances, *Fire In the Lake*. New York: Atlantic-Little, Brown, 1972. (A free-lance journalist's thoughtful analysis of the Vietnamese and the U.S. role in Vietnam)

Flanner, Janet (Genêt), *The Paris Journal* (two volumes). New York: Harcourt Brace & Jovanovich, 1977. (Drawn from her Paris reporting in *The New Yorker* from the 1920s to the 1970s)

Halberstam, David, *The Powers That Be*. New York: Knopf, 1979. (Behind the scenes at the *New York Times*)

Hellman, Lillian, *Pentimento*. New York: New American Library, 1977. (Autobiography of the writer)

Hemingway, Ernest, *A Moveable Feast*. New York: Macmillan, 1988. (Reflections on his years in Paris from 1921 to 1926)

Herr, Michael, *Dispatches*. New York: Avon, 1984. (Visceral reporting on the Vietnam War)

Hersey, John, *Hiroshima*. New York: Random House, 1985. (On the first atomic warfare)

Kessler, Lauren, and Duncan McDonald, *When Words Collide: A Journalist's Guide to Grammar and Style*. Belmont, Calif.: Wadsworth, 1984. (Thorough review of grammar)

Knightley, Phillip, *The First Casualty: From the Crimea to Vietnam: The War Correspondent as Hero, Propagandist, and Myth Maker.* New York: Harcourt, Brace & Jovanovich, 1976. (Review of twentieth-century war reporting. "The first casualty when war comes is truth")

Liebling, A. J., *The Press.* New York: Ballantine, 1975. (An acerbic media critic takes the press to task)

Mailer, Norman, *Armies of the Night.* New York: New American Library, 1971. (Anti-war demonstration at the Pentagon)

McGinnis, Joe, *The Selling of the President 1968.* New York: Trident Press, 1969. (Early attempts to use television to manipulate the public)

McPhee, John, *The John McPhee Reader.* New York: Farrar, Straus & Giroux, 1976. (Meticulous profiles of people and places)

Mitford, Jessica, *Poison Penmanship: The Gentle Art of Muckraking.* New York: Vintage, 1980. (Investigative reporting and a good introduction on her methods)

Naipaul, V. S., *An Area of Darkness.* New York: Macmillan, 1965. (Travel writing, India)

Orwell, George, *The Orwell Reader.* New York: Harcourt, Brace & Jovanovich, 1961. (Fiction, essays, and reporting)

Pirsig, Robert, *Zen and the Art of Motorcycle Maintenance.* New York: Morrow, 1979. (Physical and metaphysical travelogue)

Rosenblum, Mort, *Coups and Earthquakes: Reporting the World for America.* New York: Harper & Row, 1981. (What it's really like to be a foreign correspondent)

Ross, Lillian, *Reporting.* New York: Simon & Schuster, 1969. (Profiles of the famous and obscure, which appeared originally in *The New Yorker* in the 1940s and 1950s. It's out of print; check your library)

Schell, Jonathan, *The Fate of the Earth.* New York: Avon Books, 1982. (Reporting and analysis of the consequences of a nuclear war)

Steffens, Lincoln, *The Autobiography of Lincoln Steffens.* Volumes I and II, New York: Harcourt, Brace & World, 1958. (Late nineteenth- and early twentieth-century muckraker who uncovered political and economic corruption across the country)

Steinbeck, John, *Travels With Charley: In Search of America.* New York: Viking Press, 1962. (A man and his dog travel across America)

Stone, I. F., *The I. F. Stone Weekly Reader.* New York: Vintage, 1974. (In his one-man newsletter, Stone, for nineteen years, did some of the best investigative journalism in Washington. A collection of his analysis and reporting)

210 ◻ APPENDIX

Strunk, William, and E. B. White, *Elements of Style.* New York: Macmillan, 1979. (Principles of clarity in writing)

Talese, Gay, *The Kingdom and the Power.* New York: Dell, 1981. (The inside story on the *New York Times*)

Terkel, Studs, *Talking to Myself: A Memoir of My Times.* New York: Pantheon Books, 1977. (A memoir of one of the country's best interviewers)

Theroux, Paul, *The Great Railway Bazaar.* Boston: Houghton Mifflin, 1975. (Traveling by train through Asia)

Thomas, Lewis, *Lives of a Cell: Notes of a Biology Watcher.* New York: Bantam, 1979. ("An ode to biology")

Thompson, Hunter, *Fear and Loathing in Las Vegas.* New York: Warner Books, 1983. (*Rolling Stone*–style journalism)

A Treasury of Great Reporting: Literature Under Pressure from the Sixteenth Century to Our Own Time, edited by Louis L. Snyder and Richard B. Morris. New York: Simon & Schuster, 1962. (A classic collection of newspaper journalism from Defoe through the 1940s. It's out of print; check your library)

Tuchman, Barbara, *The Guns of August.* New York: Dell, 1962. (Historical reporting on the days and events of August 1914 and World War I)

Twain, Mark, *On Man and Beast.* Edited by Janet Smith. New York: Lawrence Hill, 1972. (A collection of his essays on animals, including "The Celebrated Jumping Frog," along with revealing biographical information on Twain)

White, E. B., *Essays of E. B. White.* New York: Harper & Row, 1979. (Eloquent, graceful essays on the minute, transitory pleasures in life)

White, Theodore, *In Search of History: A Personal Adventure.* New York: Harper & Row, 1978. (Journalist covering China, Asia, and Europe in the 1940s and 1950s for *Time Magazine*)

Wilson, Edmund, *The Portable Edmund Wilson.* New York: Penguin, 1983. (Essays on people and places, ruminations, autobiography by a journalist/man-of-letters)

Wolfe, Tom, *The New Journalism.* New York: Harper & Row, 1973. (An anthology of feature writing developed by journalists in the 1960s, along with an analysis of new journalism)

Wolfe, Tom, *The Right Stuff.* New York: Bantam, 1984. (The history of the U.S.A. Space Program)

Woodward, Bob, and Scott Armstrong, *The Brethren.* New York: Simon & Schuster, 1979. (An inside look at the Supreme Court)

Woodward, Bob, and Carl Bernstein, *All the President's Men.* New York: Simon & Schuster, 1974. (Investigative reporting that ended a Presidency)

X, Malcolm, *The Autobiography of Malcolm X.* New York: Grove Press, 1965. (On racism in America, as told to Alex Haley)

Zinsser, William, *On Writing Well.* New York: Harper & Row Perennial Library, 1988. (Style and language)

CLASSICS

For those interested in the roots of modern journalism, I suggest reading a few classic books of reportage and feature writing from several hundred to two thousand–plus years ago. It may seem strange that I propose to understand good writing in our time by going back as far as possible, to the very beginning of nonfiction, truth-based writing. But I make this proposal to give perspective on the rich tradition of journalism, and also because today's journalists are still pursuing the same goals and addressing the same ethical issues that go to the very foundations of nonfiction writing.

Caesar, Julius Caius, *The Civil War,* translated by Jane F. Mitchell. New York: Penguin, 1976. (Political autobiography, Rome's first century, B.C.)

Defoe, Daniel, *A Journal of the Plague Year,* edited by Anthony Burgess. New York: Penguin, 1966. (A novelist using the style and method of the working journalist. The great London plague of 1665)

Froissart, Jean, *Chronicles,* translated by Geoffrey Brereton. New York: Penguin, 1978. (Fourteenth-century French political reporting)

Herodotus, *The Histories,* translated by Aubrey De Selincourt. New York: Penguin, 1954. (The first attempt to collect data and give factual information on the culture, politics, and personalities of Greece and neighboring countries, fifth century, B.C.)

Machiavelli, Nicolo, *The Prince,* translated by George Bull. New York: Penguin, 1961. (Political advice and essays, in the 1600s)

Plutarch, *Plutarch's Lives,* translated by John Dryden. New York: Modern Library, 1967. (Profiles of the rich and powerful in Athens and Rome, first century, A.D.)

Polo, Marco, *The Travels of Marco Polo,* translated by Ronald Latham. New York: Penguin, 1958. (Travel writings from the Polar Sea to Java and from Zanzibar to Japan in the twelfth century, A.D.)

Thucydides, *The Peloponnesian War,* translated by Rex Warner. New York: Penguin, 1954. (Detailed reporting on the war between Athens and Sparta, fifth century, B.C.)

NOTES

INTRODUCTION

1. Rosemary L. Hake and Joseph M. Williams, "Style and Its Consequences," *College English,* vol. 43, no. 5, September 1981: p. 446.

2. Annie Dillard, *Pilgrim at Tinker Creek* (New York: Bantam, 1974), p. 35.

3. Truman Capote, *In Cold Blood* (New York: Signet, 1965), p. 15.

4. William Strunk, Jr., and E. B. White, *Elements of Style* (New York: Macmillan, 1979). Also highly recommended: Lauren Kessler and Duncan McDonald, *When Words Collide: A Journalist's Guide to Grammar and Style* (Belmont, Calif: Wadsworth, 1984).

5. George Orwell, *Collected Essays, Journalism and Letters, Vol. 4,* edited by Sonia Orwell and Ian Angus. This first appeared in *Horizon,* April 1946. (New York: Harcourt, Brace & World, 1968), pp. 138, 139.

6. Created by Roy Peter Clark, Dean of the Faculty, The Poynter Institute for Media Studies. The list, modified slightly here, appeared in elaborated form in "As Good as Their Word," *Washington Journalism Review,* February 1985. Used with permission from Roy Peter Clark.

CHAPTER 1

1. Gerald Lanson and Mitchell Stephens, "Jello Journalism: Why Reporters Have Gone Soft in Their Leads," *Washington Journalism Review*, April 1982.
2. Dirk Johnson, *New York Times*, November 2, 1987.
3. Anna Quindlen, *New York Times*, May 18, 1983.
4. Dick Roraback, Los Angeles Times Service in *International Herald Tribune*, November 12, 1987.
5. Roger Cohen, *The Wall Street Journal*, April 17, 1984.
6. William E. Geist, *New York Times*, November 28, 1984.
7. Timothy K. Smith, *The Wall Street Journal*, August 20, 1985.
8. Jan Hoffman, *Village Voice*, April 17, 1984.
9. Bob Dart, *Atlanta Journal-Constitution*, August 22, 1982.
10. Bryan Burrough, *The Wall Street Journal*, March 20, 1987.
11. Brian Ojanpa, *Free Press* (Mankato, Minn.), August 16, 1986.
12. This quote was discussed in Thomas Collins, "A Nostalgic Look at Great Leads," *Newsday*, July 7, 1982.
13. Andrew H. Malcolm, *New York Times*, October 27, 1974.
14. John Aloysius Farrell, *Denver Post*, March 4, 1982.

CHAPTER 2

1. This and the following quote are taken from Norman Sims, ed., *The Literary Journalists* (New York: Ballantine Books, 1984), p. 14. They form part of his interview with author John McPhee.
2. This term is from William Zinsser, *On Writing Well* (New York: Harper and Row, 1976).
3. Stephen Braun, *Detroit Free Press*, February 6, 1983.
4. Greta Tilley, *Greensboro News & Record* (N.C.), October 5, 1986.
5. Robert Barry, *Atlanta Journal-Constitution*, May 1, 1987.
6. Ed Breen, *Chronicle-Tribune* (Marion, Ind.), January 6, 1985.

CHAPTER 3

1. Susan Thomas, *The Tennessean*, February 8, 1987.
2. Stephen Braun, *Detroit Free Press*, October 2, 1983.
3. William Geist, *New York Times*, January 5, 1985.
4. Anna Quindlen, *New York Times*, May 18, 1983.

5. Susan Thomas and Joel Kaplan, *The Tennessean,* July 19, 1982.

6. The official definition is "to see if the searching one plans to do has already been done by someone else, especially in the preparation of a bibliography for a literature search." From Marcia J. Bates, "How to Use Information Search Tactics Online," *Online,* May 1987.

7. *Ibid.*

8. H. L. Mencken, *The American Language* (New York: Alfred A. Knopf, 1980), p. 526.

9. William Zinsser, *On Writing Well* (New York: Harper & Row Perennial Library, 1988), p. 9.

10. For more on pronouns and gender, read Dennis Baron, *Grammar and Gender* (New Haven: Yale University Press, 1986), particularly Chapter 10, "The Word that Failed," pp. 190–197.

11. H. L. Mencken, *The American Language* (New York: Alfred A. Knopf, 1980), p. 545.

12. This exercise was developed by Sonia Robbins, Assistant Professor of Journalism and Mass Communication, New York University.

CHAPTER 4

1. Related by Christopher Isherwood in George Plimpton, ed., *Writers at Work: The Paris Review Interviews,* Fourth Series (New York: Viking Press, 1976), p. 236. The Hemingway quote that leads this chapter is from the same title and page.

2. Joan Didion, "Why I Write," *New York Times Book Review,* December 5, 1976.

3. Stephen Braun, *Baltimore News American,* January 13, 1980.

4. Elizabeth Kastor, *Washington Post,* October 23, 1985.

5. Cynthia Gorney, *Washington Post,* July 24, 1987.

6. William Geist, *New York Times,* January 5, 1985.

7. Cynthia Gorney, *Washington Post,* January 4, 1984.

8. William Geist, *New York Times,* October 17, 1984.

9. Jan Hoffman, *Village Voice,* October 1, 1985.

10. Anna Quindlen, *New York Times,* March 5, 1983.

11. Roger Thurow, *Wall Street Journal,* June 28, 1984.

12. Wilmott Ragsdale, currently Professor of Journalism at the University of Puget Sound, Washington. Emphases are mine.

13. Phil Gailey, *New York Times,* August 30, 1983.

14. Greta Tilley, *Greensboro News & Record* (N.C.), March 30, 1986.

15. Ken Wells, *The Wall Street Journal,* February 7, 1984.

16. Bob Dart, *Atlanta Journal-Constitution,* August 2, 1980.

CHAPTER 5

1. Greta Tilley, *Greensboro News & Record* (N.C.), October 5, 1986.

2. Anna Quindlen, *New York Times,* May 18, 1983.

3. Neil Cunningham, *Daily Star* (Oneonta, N.Y.), June 18, 1987.

4. William Geist, *New York Times,* July 17, 1985.

5. Stan Buckles, *Rockford Register Star* (Ill.), September 7, 1984.

6. William E. Schmidt, *New York Times,* July 16, 1987.

7. Ken Miller, *Reno Gazette-Journal* (Nev.), July 14, 1985.

8. Esther B. Fein, *New York Times,* August 26, 1988.

9. Jules Loh, Associated Press, May 10, 1977.

10. John Camp, *St. Paul Pioneer Press Dispatch,* May 12, 1985.

11. Guy Trebay, *Village Voice,* October 15, 1985.

12. Cynthia Gorney, *Washington Post,* April 8, 1986.

13. Carole Agus, *Newsday,* November 6, 1984.

14. Jan Hoffman, *Village Voice,* July 27, 1982.

15. Marianne Yen, Washington Post Service, in *International Herald Tribune,* November 4, 1987.

16. Quoted in James B. Simpson, ed., *Simpson's Contemporary Quotations: The Most Notable Quotes Since 1950* (Boston: Houghton Mifflin, 1988), p. 4.

17. John Andrew, *The Wall Street Journal,* March 9, 1984.

18. William Geist, *New York Times,* December 19, 1984.

19. Nathaniel Sheppard Jr., *New York Times,* May 25, 1981.

20. Greta Tilley, *Greensboro News & Record* (N.C.), May 2, 1984.

21. Art Harris, Washington Post Service, in *Newsday,* November 6, 1984.

22. Stan Buckles, *Rockford Register Star* (Ill.), September 7, 1984.

23. Raad Cawthon, *Atlanta Journal-Constitution,* February 22, 1987.

24. Greta Tilley, *Greensboro News & Record* (N.C.), March 30, 1986.

25. Beth Mullaly, *Times-Herald Record* (Middletown, N.Y.), October 11, 1984.

26. Anna Quindlen, *New York Times,* February 26, 1983.

27. Cynthia Gorney, *Washington Post,* January 6, 1986.

28. William Geist, *New York Times,* February 29, 1984.

29. Anna Quindlen, *New York Times,* April 9, 1983.

30. John Aloysius Farrell, *Denver Post,* May 9, 1982.

31. L. Dupre Long, "In quotation, let me say . . .", *The Quill* (in which both excerpts appear), December 1980.

32. William Geist, *New York Times,* April 20, 1985.

33. Stacey Burling, *Rocky Mountain News* (Colo.), May 2, 1984.

34. Stacey Burling, *Virginian-Pilot* (Norfolk), April 30, 1981.

35. For additional suggestions on interviewing, see George M. Killenberg and Rob Anderson, *Before the Story: Interviewing and Communication Skills for Journalists* (New York: St. Martin's Press), 1989.

36. From Jessica Mitford, Introduction to *Poison Penmanship: The Gentle Art of Muckraking* (New York: Vintage, 1980), pp. 12 and 13.

CHAPTER 6

1. Molly Ivins, *New York Times,* September 30, 1976.

2. Guy Trebay, *Village Voice,* October 8, 1983.

3. Charlotte Curtis, *New York Times,* February 25, 1986.

4. Joan Didion, "Why I Write," *New York Times Book Review,* Dec. 5, 1976.

5. Both Hemingway's and Mailer's comments are from George Plimpton, ed., *Writers at Work: The Paris Review Interviews* (New York: Viking Press). Hemingway is in the Second Series, 1963, p. 239. Mailer is in the Third Series, 1967, p. 275.

6. Joan Didion, "Why I Write," *New York Times Book Review,* Dec. 5, 1976.

7. William Geist, *New York Times,* April 25, 1984.

8. Greta Tilley, *Greensboro News & Record* (N.C.), May 2, 1984.

9. Stephen Braun, *Los Angeles Times,* June 8, 1987.

10. Guy Trebay, *Village Voice,* October 2, 1984.

11. Brian Ojanpa, *Free Press* (Mankato, Minn.), November 19, 1984.

12. William Geist, *New York Times,* November 28, 1984.

13. Wesley Stout, James E. Knowles, and Angelo DeBernardo, *News and Sun-Sentinel* (Fort Lauderdale, Fla.).

14. All quotes from John McPhee appear in "Travels in Georgia," in *The John McPhee Reader* (New York: Vintage, 1977), pp. 420–471.

15. Michael T. Kaufman, *New York Times,* May 20, 1986.

16. John Hersey, *Hiroshima* (New York: Bantam, 1948), pp. 38–39 and 33–34.

17. Bob Dart, *Atlanta Journal-Constitution,* August 22, 1982.

18. Brian Ojanpa, *Free Press* (Mankato, Minn.), June 20, 1987.

19. From Michael Herr, *Dispatches* (New York: Alfred A. Knopf, 1977), pp. 56 and 57.

20. All quotes from John McPhee, "Travels in Georgia," in *The John McPhee Reader* (New York: Vintage, 1977), pp. 420–471.

21. Cynthia Gorney, *Washington Post,* July 17, 1985.

22. George Orwell called this kind of language "newspeak" in his novel *1984.* It was also called "doublethink," a way of twisting words to hide the true meaning. Life was not "bad," for instance; it was "ungood." In its January 2, 1984, issue, *U.S. News & World Report* took a look at how we measure up to Orwell's predictions about the evolution of newspeak. It turns out the language is quite unwell. Current newspeak, compiled by David A. Wiessler, includes:

Revenue enhancers: Tax increases
Reductions in force: Firing people
Negative growth: Losing, a decline
Builddown: A new arms-control plan whereby a country builds more modern missiles while at the same time tearing down its old ones
Energetic disassembly: Explosion
Rapid oxidation: Fire
Unclassified controlled information: Published material officials wish had not gotten out
Preventative imprisonment: To be held without bail, as in recent times in Argentina
Maldeployment: Being in the wrong place at the wrong time
Negative patient-care outcome: Death
Pre-need: Funeral-home lingo for buying caskets and tombstones ahead of time
Ingress activity: Space-agency talk for getting into a spacecraft
Interface: Confer, as in "I can't take any action on that until I interface with the boss"
Net-profit revenue deficiencies: Business losses
Habitability improvement: Getting comfortable

Learning process: Teaching
Adjusted behavior: Learning
Upward adjustments: Price hikes
Live on tape: One of television's favorite doublethink lines
Strategic misrepresentation: Lies

23. George Orwell, *Collected Essays, Journalism and Letters,* edited by Sonia Orwell and Ian Angus (New York: Harcourt, Brace & World, 1968), p. 134.

24. The Handy Guide to Jargon appeared in a column by Paul St. Pierre, M.P., in the *Williams Lake Tribune* (Canada), April 9, 1971.

25. Most of these redundancies are from Jim Wilkerson's article in the *Washington Journalism Review,* October 1982. A few came from the Associated Press Managing Editors Association Writing and Editing Committee.

26. From Paula LaRocque, Assistant Managing Editor and Writing Coach with the *Dallas Morning News.*

27. Jacques Barzun, *Simple and Direct: A Rhetoric for Writers* (New York: Harper & Row, 1975), p. 30.

28. For more examples and discussion of commonly confused words, see James Harrison, *Confusion Reigns: A Quick and Easy Guide to the Most Easily Mixed-Up Words* (New York: St. Martin's, 1987).

29. Desmond Morris, *The Naked Ape* (New York: McGraw-Hill, 1967), pp. 111–112.

30. For Orwell's try at this, see *Collected Essays, Journalism and Letters,* edited by Sonia Orwell and Ian Angus (New York: Harcourt, Brace & World, 1968), p. 133.

31. This exercise was developed by Sonia Robbins, Assistant Professor of Journalism and Mass Communications, New York University.

32. From the Associated Press Managing Editors Association Writing and Editing Committee. A complete list of "Fifty common errors in newspaper writing" appeared in *Editor & Publisher,* December 7, 1974. Used with permission of the Associated Press.

CHAPTER 7

1. Eugene Griffin, *Chicago Tribune,* February 5, 1973.

2. Judith Cummings, *New York Times,* November 9, 1978.

3. Stephen Braun, *Detroit Free Press,* February 6, 1983.

4. Stephen Braun, *Detroit Free Press,* February 7, 1983.

5. Nicholas Gage, *New York Times,* June 23, 1978.

6. Raad Cawthon, *Atlanta Journal-Constitution,* February 17, 1987.

7. Philip Shabecoff, *New York Times,* April 1, 1986.

8. Jim Auchmutey, *Atlanta Journal-Constitution,* June 28, 1987.

9. Cynthia Gorney, *Washington Post,* January 4, 1984.

10. John Aloysius Farrell, *Washington Post,* July 13, 1986.

11. Anna Quindlen, *New York Times,* March 9, 1983.

12. Bob Dart, *Atlanta Journal-Constitution,* August 22, 1982.

13. Keith Graham, *Atlanta Journal-Constitution,* March 10, 1987.

14. Greta Tilley, *Greensboro News & Record* (N.C.), October 5, 1986.

15. Stephen Braun, *Detroit Free Press,* February 7, 1983.

16. John Aloysius Farrell, *News American* (Baltimore), May 10, 1981.

17. Raad Cawthon, *Atlanta Journal-Constitution,* February 15, 1987.

18. Nick Ravo, New York Times Service in *International Herald Tribune,* December 7, 1987.

19. William Geist, *New York Times,* June 22, 1985.

20. Cynthia Gorney, *Washington Post,* July 17, 1985.

21. Anna Quindlen, *New York Times,* October 24, 1983.

22. Guy Trebay, *Village Voice,* October 15, 1985.

23. Susan Thomas, *The Tennessean,* December 21, 1981.

CHAPTER 8

1. The basic concept was developed by Donald Murray, writing coach and columnist, *The Boston Globe.* The concept was presented and discussed at the Poynter Institute for Media Studies, St. Petersburg, Fl., during a May, 1983, seminar for journalism teachers attended by the author and co-sponsored by the American Society of Newspaper Editors.

2. Anna Quindlen, "Times Talk" (the in-house publication of the *New York Times*). February, 1983.

3. Both Mailer's and Hemingway's writing habits are described in detail in George Plimpton, ed., *Writers at Work: The Paris Review Interviews* (New York: Viking Press). Mailer is in the Third Series, pp. 257–259. Hemingway is in the Second Series, pp. 217–225.

4. John Leonard, *New York Times,* September 2, 1977.

5. David Huddle, *New York Times Book Review,* January 31, 1988.

6. Most of these descriptions were adapted from Eugene Sheehy, ed., *Guide to Reference Books* 10th ed. (Chicago: American Library Association, 1986).

CHAPTER 10

1. This is adapted from the suggested Letter of Agreement of the American Society of Journalists and Authors, copyright 1979.

2. Melissa Ludtke Lincoln, *Columbia Journalism Review*, September/October 1981.

3. Terri (Schultz) Brooks, *Columbia Journalism Review*, January/February 1984. The material and quotes on page 199–202 appeared originally in this article. For additional readings on authors' rights, the author suggests her article, "Writers Equity: Time for a National Union?", *The Quill*, October, 1982.

INDEX